ADVENTURES IN SELF-DISCOVERY

The Journey from Mind to Heart to Consciousness

ADVENTURES IN SELF-DISCOVERY
The Journey from Mind to Heart to Consciousness
Copyright © Srinivas Arka 2000

All Rights Reserved

No part of this book may be reproduced in any form,
by photocopying or by any electronic or mechanical means,
including information storage or retrieval systems,
without permission in writing from both the copyright owner
and the publisher of this book.

Humble Books
P.O. Box 2217
London W1A 5GZ
United Kingdom

Humble Books
Printed in England

ADVENTURES IN SELF-DISCOVERY

The Journey from Mind to Heart to Consciousness

Srinivas Arka

Humble Books
Mayfair, London W1

As flowers blossom in sunshine,
So does the Inner-Self blossom in Silence.

Silence is the true nature of Consciousness.

Sound is the nature of the Body.

Life exists between Sound and Silence.

Silence is the Melody of Life.

When you are out of Melody,
Life becomes chaotic, confusing and complex.

Spiritual inspiration brings one's Life of Melody
Back onto the floor of Harmony
Where Love and Bliss are special effects.

Srinivas Arka

CONTENTS

Part One
The Physical Self

Chapter 1 ~ *Self-Realisation ~ Life Beyond the Physical Senses* 12

Chapter 2 ~ *Conscious Health* 17

Chapter 3 ~ *Success and Failure* 22

Chapter 4 ~ *The Semi-earthly Mind and the Spiritual Heart* 29

Chapter 5 ~ *Fission and Fusion* 35

Chapter 6 ~ *Positivity and Negativity ~ The Dual Unfoldment of the Cosmic Seed* 39

Part Two
The Emotional Self

Chapter 7 ~ *Emotion ~ A Direct Expression of the Heart* 50

Chapter 8 ~ *Love ~ Living the Fullness of Life* 53

Chapter 9 ~ *Love and Lust* 56

Chapter 10 ~ *Courage and Fear* 66

Chapter 11 ~ *Misery and Happiness* 71

Part Three
Personal Expression

Chapter 12 ~ *Smile ~ A Sign of Joy* 78
Chapter 13 ~ *Naturalness and Artificiality* 83
Chapter 14 ~ *Pride and Vanity* 87
Chapter 15 ~ *Admiration and Flattery* 90
Chapter 16 ~ *Humility and Arrogance* 94
Chapter 17 ~ *Humour and Seriousness* 98
Chapter 18 ~ *Gratitude ~ Pathway to Bliss and Realisation* 104
Chapter 19 ~ *Respect ~ The Gesture of a True Human Being* 108

Part Four
The Quest

Chapter 20 ~ *Question and Inquiry* 115
Chapter 21 ~ *Clarity and Confusion* 118
Chapter 22 ~ *Intelligence and Intuition* 122
Chapter 23 ~ *The Art of Walking Backwards (Internally)* 130

Part Five
Direct Spirituality

Chapter 24 ~ *From Silence to Sound ~ From Sound to Silence* 137

Chapter 25 ~ *Silence ~ The True Nature of Consciousness* 141

Chapter 26 ~ *The Meeting of Heart and Mind* 145

Chapter 27 ~ *Merging the Wave of Life with the Ocean of Consciousness* 148

Chapter 28 ~ *Sit, Sit, Sit* 152

Part Six
The Curve of Spirituality

Chapter 29 ~ *The Sweetness of Words* 158

Chapter 30 ~ *Words, Meaning, Mother (Ma)* 163

Chapter 31 ~ *Desire ~ Dream of the Awakened Mind* 167

Chapter 32 ~ *Your Mystic Space* 169

Chapter 33 ~ *Time from the Timeless* 173

Chapter 34 ~ *Miracles* 176

Chapter 35 ~ *The Cosmic Tree* 179

Chapter 36 ~ *The Triangle of Life* 184

Chapter 37 ~ *Dhyana ~ Experiencing and Understanding the Invisible Side of Life and the Universe* 187

Chapter 38 ~ *Life is Consciousness and Consciousness is Life* 193

Glossary **198**

Part One
The Physical Self

The senses do not have their own individual, conscious existence.

Take eyeglasses, for example. You wear them. You see through them, yet they have no individual conscious existence. Even if you wear a contact lens or implant a lens permanently into your eye, it is still lifeless. It assists you, but *you* remain the operator and owner. And *you* see through the lens. *You* are superior to it and add meaning to it. You create eyeglasses by giving them a certain shape. *You* use them and wear them but you are far from the truth if you believe your eyeglasses are your eyes. You can take them off at any time. There are those who may believe that eyeglasses are part of their physical existence, like one of their bodily limbs. You can observe this in people who have worn glasses for some time. In the beginning, when they first wore glasses, they could not turn their heads naturally, as though the glasses controlled their movements. They took time to become accustomed to the glasses. Soon they felt no difference between their glasses and their eyes.

Similarly, for those who have not realised themselves, the senses are everything to them. Eyes cannot see on their own. They only help you see. Eyes are like naturally fixed glasses that remain with you throughout your life. You are the one who sees. If you don't see, your eyes become lifeless. Our physical eyes have many limitations. With them, you can see only up to a certain distance and no further. A speck of dust can be enough to blur your vision. When you look in one direction, you cannot see behind you, or in any other direction. If you look at a very bright light, you have an overwhelming urge to close your eyes. There are many limitations to your physical eyes, but *you* are the seer. Your eyes are very helpful, but they are merely instruments for you to see through.

If your eyes are closed while wearing eyeglasses, you cannot see anything. When you are absorbed in thinking seriously about something, you cannot see what is happening in front of you, even though your eyes are open. This means that you, as the seer, are otherwise occupied and not present in your own eyes at that moment. At such times, the eyes are useless. There is no difference between you and a person who is blind or blindfolded. Similarly, when you listen to something very intently, you cannot see clearly. Even if you see, you cannot remember what you have seen, because the mind has shifted from the eyes to the ears.

While watching television, the mind alternates between the auditory and the visual senses, and the brain weaves these two different kinds of information into one single idea. You don't even notice this because these shifts happen so quickly. There are many limitations to our senses, because they are just instruments. We cannot manage our lives without using them consciously. Most humans have still not delved into the deeper layers of 'consciousness' in order to solve the riddles of the senses, intellect, mind, body and the spirit.

Those who are born blind see with their inner eye, much like – or perhaps even better than – a person with full eyesight. Others may not believe this, but the blind experiencer can confirm this truth. Others may be deaf, but they can still hear their inner melody. They understand different patterns of music through directing their consciousness to follow and understand sound vibrations. The senses have limitations. One cannot understand the profundity of life when wholly depending on them.

Stretching and projecting one's consciousness to a higher altitude is spiritual ascension. Then the past, present and future, along with various other facets of our existence, can be surveyed. This cannot be achieved while we live only on a sensory level. It can happen only when one's level of comprehension rises above the senses, synchronizing one's energies with the projection of consciousness. Only then is it possible to reach the peak of life and understand its wholeness.

Take a cone-shaped object. Pour oil on its apex. The oil will circle down and cover the whole area. It may take some time, but it will surely cover the total surface of the cone. When you reach such a great height as to see the full dimension of life, the experience that you achieve is equally distributed over all areas of life. Energy is distributed. Knowledge is dispersed. Consciousness spreads throughout the cone of your being. If one can understand and realise this, everything in the universe can be clearly visualised. Nothing will remain enigmatic.

For example, imagine meeting someone coming from another city. If you analyse the person's speech, style, and mannerisms, you can draw conclusions about what that city looks like, its level of civilisation, customs, culture and so on. If you are a keen observer, you see all these things. So, also, when you realise the very meaning and significance of life, there is nothing left in the cosmos to be understood. That is realisation. That is complete realisation. Then you become light. No trace of shadow, or hue of negativity, can be seen thereafter. You extend and grow in many directions and many forms, even though you are confined to your physical body. Joy becomes the testimony of such an attainment. Such a way of living establishes spiritual realisation, or realisation of the Self.

Whether people accept you or not, you are a realised *atma*, a realised conscious entity. Nothing distracts you from experiencing joy within. Now and then, just for a change, you may come to the surface to peep out and see what is happening in the world. At that moment, you may feel slightly disturbed if there is a materialistic storm or mental chaos. Then, you would descend and touch your being to reconfirm, 'Yes, I am pure consciousness.' You take this message deep into your heart and never forget it, because this memory, impression and self-reminder shields you against negative influences. You will not lack anything required to make your life complete and successful. Internally you are rich and comfortable. Circumstances come and go like clouds, but you are not affected or influenced by them. You shine like a sun. Although there is a screen of clouds in front of you, you remain silent and steadfast until the clouds of circumstances pass. After a few moments you are back to yourself.

Those who are unrealised and unspiritual are mostly manipulated by circumstances. Their individuality is very much affected. They live as if they are the senses, without conscious projection. They become victims of their own circumstances, which is worse than being a puppet. At least a puppet is handled by human hands, but here external circumstances are in full control. A realised *atma*, on the other hand, achieves an overall vision and view of his or her own life.

Realisation of the Self is not the same in everyone, because the dimension of each life differs. It also depends on one's personal evolution of consciousness. Some people are physically old, but spiritually young. Others are spiritually old, but look young physically. It is of vital importance to understand, as well as experience, the depth of our being, and there is no justifiable excuse for delaying this noble task. Until you have understood your own life, at least to some degree, you are not qualified to understand and empathise, understand and communicate with others on a deeper level. Allow yourself to experience your life's fullness. It is a process that does not happen overnight. It requires immense patience. You will know when it flashes within you. Once you have embarked upon this inner spiritual journey, it is certain that at some time, Self-realisation will dawn on you.

When you are consciously able to discern between energy and matter, you are superior to these two cosmic states of existence. This is the beauty of the human consciousness. When this fact is realised – 'Oh, I am this, let me explore' – then experiences begin to occur in the field of consciousness. In the course of such inner love experiences, you manifest your love in many ways. You give out that energy without your own knowledge. Others who come into your field of radiation feel the flow of that energy of love from you. Both the transmitter and the receiver experience that circulation of energy simultaneously. It is love. It is a reality, but those who embrace only technical thinking have difficulty accepting it as love.

One could call it a flow of energy, a field of force, a wholesome emotional bath, or a shared, positive, psychophysical exchange and experience. In love, your heart opens up. Your mind settles. Your body bounces with joy. It is conscious and spiritual. It can be experienced, but not explained. Even the lengthiest explanation would only be like a preface to the actual experience. And with this experience, great miracles happen. You dance without being taught. You sing beautifully without taking lessons. You write excellently without being a writer. And all because you have awakened your love. You recognise the same love even in strangers. People who feel negative may approach you, but the power of love radiating from you is such that they calm down, and find it impossible to be negative around you.

Inspiration wakes up this love. It is not restricted to any particular racial, religious or national backgrounds, but is universal. The process of this internal exploration of love is mystical. There is no need to convince others about this awakening of love in you. (Many are only interested in convincing others rather than convincing themselves.) If you have had this experience, your words naturally become authentic, because they come directly from your heart. Your biological and intellectual existence, and that nothing exists beyond that. They lose themselves in mere scientific thinking and live out their lives far from their own true consciousness.

When we close our eyes, we can see and experience the phenomena of the physical universe, objects, and even distances in the same way as when our eyes are open. In this way, we absorb all that comes within our sight into our inner being. In order to accommodate these images in us we need a different kind of space than the space outside of us. In this space within us, we can rebuild and restore a myriad of impressions and experiences. This space is not the space we see outside. It is a conscious, mystic space that is not interwoven with the external dimensions of time and space.

Modern man puts his emphasis on receiving information from the outside world. One may think for a moment, *'Where am I able to store these things in me? Do I have that much space?'* Instead, time is spent gathering information from outside, rather than making space to receive inspiration from within. The health of our inner consciousness can be achieved only when the sleeping love is awakened within, by the clapping together of the heart and consciousness. There is no set external exercise for this; it is an internal effort, which is done in solitude.

Every individual is born with this conscious power. We are the highest form of conscious entity on earth. We have all the qualities of representing the ongoing, ever-expanding eternal cosmos. Physically, we may change our forms and shapes, but internally we are the same cosmic beings. Five million years ago we were the same, and we will continue to remain the same. Respecting the laws of evolution, we may grow old and cast off the carnal cover, but we are sure to obtain new attire or dress, according to the location of our habitation in space. *Even if you consider yourself gas, liquid, solid or a combination of matter and energy, you will continue to exist, since matter and energy are indestructible in nature.*

physical problems, but deep inside such people feel an inexplicable discomfort that is incurable by medical means alone. That internal sickness is solid and difficult to dissolve or break up. They may go for all kinds of treatment but there is no cure, because the root cause of their ill health is not just physical or mental; therefore, chemical or psychiatric treatment is unable to fully address the condition. Only experienced, spiritually evolved people can give comfort and a sense of relief from such metaphysical sickness. In these cases, going to the core of one's being becomes absolutely necessary. Inner consciousness can bloom only when love is realised spiritually, rather than analysed theoretically and mentally. When consciousness is bathed in love, negative characteristics like envy, hatred and jealousy are flushed out. As a consequence, the mind regains its positive attitude, subsequently bringing positive changes in the body.

Love is the ultimate self-treatment for everyone's total well-being. All species are born with love. All the cosmic laws and forces are in complete love with one another. All heavenly bodies are held in their positions because of the gravity of love. You become so warm and sweet when such love is awakened. You cannot ask someone for such love, because it is an inner self-experience.

Love is energy. It is a force – sometimes very subtle like the wind; at other times, solid and strong like a mountain. It has a curative effect on both body and mind. One can exercise such love only when one is determined to expand one's consciousness. To experience this otherwise dormant love, mystical inspiration is necessary. With it, you see beyond visual boundaries, and even hear inaudible sounds internally. You become a recipient of the subtle messages given by nature. Love overflows, and every cell in the body feels and shares the experience. Love has such a powerful and positive influence. Most people are sceptical about their own spiritual existence. They believe themselves to be limited only to a

2
Conscious Health

Health means a feeling of painlessness and an experience of unity within and without. The after-effect of this is joy, courage, peace and the confidence of well-being. Our health is related not only to our physical well-being, but also to sound mind and the wellness of something beyond body and mind, which dwells within us. That is conscious health.

Intense research is being carried out to trace the reasons and cures for diseases, yet this has met with little success. Until recently, scientific thinking had increasingly reinforced the idea, 'I am the body.' That 'I' means the physical existence. In searching for answers though, science has been compelled to study, experiment and develop the 'mind over body' theory. Only within the past few decades has the realisation dawned that most diseases are psychosomatic. Treatments given from this perspective still seem very clinical and mechanical, and they often exacerbate the condition rather than relieve or alleviate it.

People suffering from mental and physical disorders, and other 'dis-eases' caused mostly by the pressures of social and personal life, are now looking for alternative methods and cures. However, *one of the most effective cures for any negative condition is the awakening of love.*

Health of consciousness is the root of everyone's well-being. If inner consciousness shrinks, grace, beauty and vitality dwindle. Some people may appear normal from the outside, and physicians may certify that they have no joy and love express themselves through your smile and appearance. Love becomes a thread that weaves your body, mind and conscious Self into wholeness. This shields and equips you to withstand any kind of situation. The waves of your consciousness are in full force and cannot wither. Your heart feels more tenderness. Your body gains comfort. Your mind becomes your best friend. You realise that your physical existence is simply a centre with consciousness gracefully circling it, powered by the force of love. And with this love, consciousness enjoys spiritual health, which then ripples and resounds throughout the body and mind.

3
Success and Failure

Humankind is inevitably tossed between the regularly occurring polarities of success and failure. Success is considered to be a cause for celebration, and failure a cause for sorrow. One who has opened the spiritual eye celebrates inner joy and avoids being affected by the oscillation of success and failure. However, materialists continue to suffer at both extremes, even though they may seem delighted by success. Success is only a superficial joy. With failure, people face a difficult solitary trial, which is actually an opportunity for the re-examination of their priorities. Failure is a gateway to a new life, inviting one to retreat inwards, and educating one to become strong and sound.

Human life is a network of intricacies and complexities. Humanity is pitched between two major aspects of life. One is success and the other is failure. Success and failure are like love and lust, and like the crest and trough of a wave. They can also be compared to day and night. Success is like explanation and offers only transient pleasure, whereas failure is like experience and holds a hidden message.

When you achieve success, you enjoy only a small portion of it. The rest is interpreted, valued and judged by others.

Success is like a guest who walks into your house with many colourful gifts, bringing sudden cheer and exuberance. You are entertained, as if with some new, sensational news. Your relationship with success is intoxicating, tempting and ephemeral. Today it is here, but tomorrow it is gone. Failure, on the other hand, is a true friend, who stays longer.

In success, one is tempted with egoism, self-centredness and fanaticism, but not so with failure. Failure helps one to become an introvert, a great thinker and a philosopher. In failure you withdraw all the links of your being from the external world and look within. The effect of failure can be profound, but success does not inspire you in this way. In success, you become an extrovert, because it invites you further into the outside world. You forget your individuality and become involved in the intricacies of external life. However, when success is achieved *after* passing through failure, you can truly enjoy and cherish it, because you have been moulded into a better personality by the furnace of experience. Now you can wear success without becoming vain.

Success is seductive and maintains a precarious balance, much as if you are standing on the edge of a cliff. If your attention is diverted, even for a moment, you are in danger of falling. One wrong step and success loses its grip on you. It becomes increasingly strenuous to maintain your success. You must continuously be on guard, aware of your posture, position, mood and the condition of both your body and mind. Onlookers may appreciate your success from a distance, but they don't know how difficult it is to maintain.

Failure can be compared to a person standing on safe, flat ground. There is no danger, and nowhere to go except upward.

Our mind misinterprets the meaning of failure, just as it misinterprets birth and death. Birth is considered a success by most people today and death a failure but, for the conscious Self, it is seen as the opposite. Few warm up to this idea.

Death is a success for the inner conscious Self, since it attains freedom from the confinement created by the elements in nature. The interpretation of the mind tends to be opposite to that of the conscious Self. The mind has an immense desire to maintain its existence within the physical body, because it is formed along with the birth of the physical body, much like a bubble forms in water. The mind sees death as total failure. As time progresses, the sense in which death is understood may change – it may be seen as a transition into a different dimension of existence. For those on a spiritual path it is an unassailable truth. It is neither a success nor a failure, but simply being (past), being (present), being (future).

Success in life inevitably brings insidious after-effects with it. These may be temptations for tomorrow's downfall, or snares to imprison you in the trap of utter materialism. Those who are spiritually inspired are aware of the consequences of the material trap. Materialistic people suffer, whether they succeed or fail. When they achieve something, they become egocentric and are unable to listen to other people's advice. Their minds are blocked. They believe that success will go on forever, and they try to impose their ideas on others. They ignorantly hoist the flag of overconfidence, and invest dogmatic ideas into the future. You can clearly note both vanity and grimness on their faces. Such success is grasped covetously and cannot be success from a spiritual point of view.

Worldly success may be achieved by great effort, or just through a stroke of luck. It may be in a profession, education, sports, business or any other field. Such success is superficial, and those who succeed are possessive and claim all the credit.

Although they try to hold on to it, it is fleeting, like an ice cube held in the hand. With the ice cube, you lose any way you choose. You can throw it away now and lose it, or you can hold on to it, numbing your hands, until it melts away and is gone.

When people experience failure, it is a complete failure of life. It is a failure of the mind, failure of the family, failure of the world, failure of everything. In addition, they become narrow-minded and pessimistic. Their negativity, anger and cynicism spreads to others. Even if they are successful, they drag others into unnecessary competition and provoke their hidden jealousy. So also in failure, they become extremely depressed and disappointed, because their efforts were materialistic, and only projected to achieve an intended result in a calculated way. They are not prepared to accept and handle the incident with circumspection. There is no patience and prudence. There is no spiritual understanding – it is just a process, an exercise in obstinacy. They are not prepared to accept the truth because they expected only success.

When these 'success-minded' people fail, they collapse into negativity. Some may even suffer a nervous breakdown. When success is achieved by people who are purely materialistic, it cannot bring peace and prosperity because they do not possess deserving qualities and so are not qualified to handle it. On the other hand, if success is achieved consciously and received gracefully, your mind and energies are focused, but you are also open-minded and open-hearted. You are deserving, and therefore welcome, enjoy and cherish it. In this case success is not just a temporary guest, but a permanent lover. This success remains with you although you do not try to possess it.

Real success comes involuntarily to those who are assiduous. They make their best efforts according to their beliefs, knowledge and capacities, following the laws of nature and respecting the limitations of a changing world.

They are open-minded about the outcome, and appreciate and welcome both failure and success equally. When success comes, it does not trigger egoism, self-centredness, possessiveness or other negative qualities, because all who have assisted and co-operated, directly or indirectly, are appreciated and acknowledged. Now success is a natural and spiritual celebration, whether it is an individual success, a family success or the success of many others. Whole-hearted thankfulness is extended to each and every individual who genuinely tendered his or her goodwill for the achievement. There is no room for jealousy because many are involved.

The role of such success is played humbly and simply, in that the success is acknowledged as belonging to everyone. Your success is everyone's success and everyone's joy. You become a caretaker of the success and, even if you forget to protect it, others will look after it because of their ethical and emotional involvement. Hence, it is a collective and spiritual success. It inspires others, providing an unspoken example to everyone. You expand the family of success, and both you and others progress.

You do not lose hope or confidence when you fail, but actually learn many things. You look deeply into the situation, exploring and examining the reasons for the failure. You do not become depressed, because you know you made your best effort. You take responsibility for the outcome, not blaming others, but looking to see how you alone can improve from the lesson. You want to experience the wholeness of it, so that the failure becomes a concrete foundation for your future. You become a researcher. Is it a social failure? Is it a domestic, economic or psychological failure? Is it really a failure at all? Now is the time you test family, friends and others – by how they react and behave, when they perceive you as having failed. Do they desert or criticise you? You fully feel, experience and contemplate all these aspects and more, using intuition and consciousness.

You learn from the experience, so as not to repeat it. The next time, you will be prepared for any type of obstacle or hindrance. You make your journey smoother and safer because of this research.

Rather than despairing, you bring your total awareness to focus on the situation. You rise above the ordinary state of the mind, so as to enjoy the failure internally and spiritually, in a mystical way. It ennobles you and you rejoice. In success, you involve others by sharing it and your joy, while in failure, you become the sole custodian, taking full responsibility and making no excuses.

Because for you failure is a beautiful experience, you still look composed and calm, and evolve and progress because of it. You may even share the real experience of failing by talking or writing a book or essay about how it helped you grow. This can contribute a great deal to others, who may be in similar difficulties without the benefit of your experience.

In deeper understanding and experiencing of the inner Self, success and failure are intertwined into a single thread, and you drop that thread through the mind and deep down to the conscious level. No matter what the mind says, you don't listen to it. Instead, the mind listens to you, and becomes your friend and student. It does not matter whether you are on marshy or panoramic ground, you simply enjoy what life brings you. So you remain unperplexed, developing an empathy and understanding for everyone, everything and for every event and turn of your life. Your inner peace and satisfaction are maintained in winter or summer, rain or sunshine. You experience life's warmth and an expansion of consciousness. Success is like the bright moon. Failure is like the dark moon. The reality is that the moon is neither dark nor bright. What we see of it is only a reflection of the sun. You are the sun. You shine spiritually on everything in life equally. You remain unperturbed, safe and sound, rising above the constraints of success and failure, thus making your life a *real* success.

4
The Semi-earthly Mind and the Spiritual Heart

The physical body is purely a tangible body, absolutely a visible existence. This form of existence is earthly. The mind is semi-physical or semi-earthly, whereas the inner conscious Self is by nature invisible and spiritual. A fine cosmic combination of these three ingredients gives rise to a beautiful human entity. If you visualise the conscious Self as the ocean, then the mind is its waves. It is impossible to find an ocean without waves.

There cannot be any manifestation of the conscious Self without there being a mind. You may cut your nails, trim your hair, take off your clothes, change your name, but you cannot escape from the fetters of the mind. The mind is like translucent smoke, an entity, not quite visible within oneself. Its tremendous influence on one's life cannot be ruled out. The brain is its prime field of activity. Though the mind pervades the whole body, it manifests predominantly in the brain.

The mind can be compared to a film projectionist. The mind makes the brain its projector and projects its own whims and fantasies. Although there is no literal screen within the cortex's nervous system, you watch many things as a spectator when you close your eyes. You also may lose control of your own projections. Rather than you directing the mind, the mind directs you.

Those who are spiritually aware, or those who have spiritual understanding and experience, can overcome the mind's influence to a great degree. Others find it difficult to cross the mind's boundary and escape from its clutches. Such people may also become prisoners of their own minds. That is often why those who let their minds run their lives cannot experience love or cannot visualise their path in life.

You can either go beneath the mind or beyond it. It is paradoxical that either way you will reach your consciousness, but it is easier to go beneath the mind. The mind also exists between physics and metaphysics. It can switch or be switched in any direction. This is because the human mind can adapt itself to various ways of learning. Knowing merely the workings and chemistry of one's brain, it is not always possible to determine what one is thinking or what one could think. Although the brain is the abode of the mind, the mind is far different from the brain.

One can only tame or subdue its behaviour. It is not possible to cease the mind, or to arrest it, but it is possible to ease it.

By following various physical techniques in meditation, you can explore the mind, but this does not reveal the deep-seated inner conscious spirit. The body is like a machine or a robot. It has its infrastructural mechanism, and it can be studied, analysed and understood technically. But the mind cannot be treated technically or mathematically because it is a subjective and abstract concept and experience.

The mind wants to impose or transmit its impressions on you, so the moment you close your eyes, pictures start appearing, one after another. Nobody can say precisely what a person is going to think next. That is the nature of the mind. People who are caught up in their minds are unsettled and cannot find peace. The mind is their whole existence and life seems like a desert. No matter how much they achieve, they do not find satisfaction and inner bliss. They exert a great deal of energy to gain material wealth, yet they do not find what they want because of the mind's influence. Some even become sceptics.

If you go beneath the mind, you see the same as when you go beyond it. When you go beyond the mind you ascend on a macrocosmic scale. When you go beneath the mind, you descend into the deeper levels of your microcosmic existence. Since your inner wishes are always genuine, they are unaffected by normal worldly limitations. The heart is an immensely sensitive centre of your being that filters all negativity coming from the mind. When you become the heart, you become the director and you turn the mind towards positive action.

It is very healthy and safe to go beneath the mind and journey to the centre of your conscious Self, which is very close and accessible to you. The journey is mystical and the vehicle unknown, but you can reach your destination. This pilgrimage is long and interesting. You not only perceive the truth about yourself, but also your destiny, your future activity and the wholeness of your being. You see with your third or inner eye, which exists between the physical eyes.

The moment you close your physical eyes, you see many things. This means the mind has started operating its projector. Images keep coming. Some are logically explainable, some are out of control and others are out of your reach, but the images still keep coming. If you can focus a bit more, in time the appearance and disappearance of those images gradually slows down. After a while images become much clearer. Just remain an observer without getting involved rationally. Do not attempt to interpret them. Now, images lead you into details. In those details you may find some reminders, answers or tips for solutions to problems. You think or feel, 'This is enough,' and with a blink you are back to the physical vision. The mind returns to its surface activity.

Then you wake up and say, 'Oh, where was I?' You were here all the time. What you saw with your inner eye was only a blurred vision because it was covered in karmic dust, or impressions, from all the information that has been accumulated during your lifetime, or some information that may have crept in from pre-existence. Such information just unfurls.

You become tired because you lose energy – more energy than a person who does hard physical labour. When you are agitated, energies are released from your being like arrows, multi-directionally. You become exhausted within a few minutes. This is more than exhaustion, more than regular tiredness, and it may take many days or months for you to renew your energy.

When you slowly descend beneath the mind, energy may still be expended from body and mind, but to a smaller degree. You gain different kinds of energies that are absorbed by your own inner conscious spirit, and are stored somewhere within you in the form of subtle impressions. When you gradually go beneath the mind, with the inspiration you receive from your faith or any other sources, you can harness your mind and energies. You discover much comfort within you, because you are spiritually aware of your existence. Nothing is missing in your life. You will touch or embrace everything that makes life beautiful and comfortable. You develop the ability to absorb goodness, truth and love from the universe. You have no regrets. If you are only materialistic from identifying only with the mind, then you will have regrets at every stage of life, saying, 'I wish I had done this' and 'I wish I had gained that.' You will keep complaining about yourself, about nature and about those around you. Your path in life is lost and you subside into a negative existence.

When spiritual and material existence are in balance, life's journey can be smooth and safe. Through an internal search, you can achieve this. You may not be able to explain exactly the way you feel inside, since that is your private experience. It does not matter whether you go into the inner regions of your heart for a second or for an hour. It is the quality of the experience that matters, and not the duration.

Each time you are in that state, you understand, or realise, your multifaceted existence in different regions of the universe. Yesterday you were in another place, and tomorrow you will be in a different place. Now, sitting here today, you can sense those impressions that were held on the magnetic field at yesterday's location, and you can reconnect with them. One day, as your being continues to expand in this manner, you will become ubiquitous with your consciousness.

The purpose of understanding and experiencing the full dimension of life is to gain complete positivity or illumination, following which there will be no doubt, no darkness, no negativity and no fear. That is the ultimate goal. You go to spiritually developed people to confirm that you, too, are evolving in that dimension. You want to refresh your vision and re-establish yourself as a spiritual being, confirming that you are more than just human.

So you go to a spiritual teacher to experience the feeling of being uplifted by waves of energy and touch. When you re-emerge, your friends may ask you, "What have you achieved?" You cannot explain it in words, and you simply smile. Your smile is meaningful, and conveys more than you would say. It is a spiritual smile, indicating the emergence of new life, the blossoming of your consciousness and the unfolding of your personality. You smile because you have realised that you are a blissful spiritual being.

The individual mind usually demonstrates a bipolar effect, which interprets words and actions as right or wrong, pleasant or unpleasant, painful or pleasurable. One person interprets this one way, while another interprets it in a different way. Both are effects of the mind. It is like a jigsaw puzzle, in which all the different facets, even seemingly contradictory aspects, fit together.

The moment you translate your thoughts into feelings, you escape the tentacles of the mind. How is this done? There is no physical route or map to guide you. It is a unique, mystical and internal pathway, a beautiful and cosmic journey. Now, we are at the dawn of the twenty-first century. The age of mind is over. The age of consciousness is dawning. Scientists, philosophers, artists and spiritual teachers will work together to discover the infinite powers of consciousness. This is a good sign. The mind-approach will become outdated and obsolete within a few decades. This will be another stage of evolution. Each person has an important role in expanding his or her consciousness, and creating a new evolutionary life in the life of the universe.

5
Fission and Fusion

The splitting of energies is generally destructive and disharmonious. Unification of energies is generally constructive and harmonious. We are gifted to operate our energies either way.

The atom is unimaginably insignificant in its physical size, even when compared to the smallest visible speck of dust. Even though scientists have never seen an atom, its power is very significant. If you consider humans only as biological beings, they are insignificant in their existence. If you consider a human being as a biological being with a special faculty called the mind, human existence is still insignificant. Any hypnotist can put you in a trance and make a puppet out of you. You simply listen to his commands. A psychic can read your mind to a degree. If you have a slight discomfort or pain in the body you cannot concentrate, and you may not be happy at your work or with people. Anyone can put sedatives in your drink and make you sleep. Anyone can disturb your mind very easily. So how significant is your existence?

If you consider yourself superior to your mind, then you are a recognisable human species. When you discover you are a conscious being and that mind and body are just the limbs of your being, then you are eligible to comprehend the incomprehensible. Everyone is born pure since nature is pure but as we grow, as we develop our intellect, we gather something from the world that is unwanted, disturbing and negative into our life and mind. The only way to discover or rediscover the innate purity of our existence is to deepen our consciousness into the inmost recesses of our being through spiritual means. So, as we go deeper and deeper into our mind, into our heart, into our consciousness and into our being, we become aware that we are born pure and that we are pure conscious beings. Nothing can soil our natural beauty or the innocence and originality of our nature or being. In this process, we do not just become aware of our purity; instead, we regain this through personal, mystical and spiritual experiences. Then no one can hypnotise us. Those who believe that life is merely a psychological or biological existence are more vulnerable because they have no protective qualities with which to establish their existence, or to protect themselves against invasion from destructive elements in nature.

No one can disturb you easily when you become aware that you are superior to your mind. Your inner peace, individuality and self-awareness cannot be disturbed by anyone or by anything in the universe. You may show a sign of discomfort, pain or agony as a reaction when someone interferes with your being, but you remain undisturbed internally. The existence of the atom in the physical sense is insignificant because you cannot see it or feel its touch. It is significant, however, because of the abundant energy in itself. When nuclei are split by the process of fission, they release energies such as thermal energy, gamma rays and so on.

Similarly, the ego is the nucleus of a person. If it is provoked, irritated or attacked, the ego splits, negative energy is released and thoughts emerge that are malevolent or penetrating. You can feel the negative energy surrounding or being released from people like this if you are standing close to them. They become very destructive. Even though they usually look physically weak, at this moment of anger and extreme agitation they manifest a great release of negative energy. They may break something or attack another person, sometimes without being aware of their own actions and their consequences.

If the nuclei fuse in the process called nuclear fusion, a substantial amount of energy is released. This can also result in the formation of heavier metals. Philosophically, fusion results in a positive effect. Fission results in a negative outcome. When you fuse your mind, energy, body and all the resources available within you with love, you become strong and positive. Fusion is always constructive – a spiritual attitude to bring different things into oneness. Fission is destructive if it is not utilised in the right sense.

When the ego of a person is split, as a nucleus is split in fission, the person splits from friends and family. The person also drifts from spiritual understanding. In fusion, the person comes close to people. Such people can bring about transformation in others. They can also unite broken families, creating the experience of harmony and oneness.

If you are spiritually inclined, you believe in constructiveness and always work in that direction. You become strong and you strengthen your family and surroundings as well. You become an architect. Splitting may be very easy, but its effect is difficult to erase. It leaves a long-lasting negative impression upon a person, and there is no effective external treatment to cure one from ailments arising from negative impressions, because only the individual himself or herself can effect the shift and cure. Even the very thought of splitting creates problems in oneself.

Human life is like an atom. Where is the human in this universe, when the solar system itself is negligible in the vast expanses of the universe? Just like a grain of sand on a seashore. Where does the individual fit in? Only because of 'conscious' awareness can the individual become prominent and significant.

You can reach anywhere and feel any object or species with your conscious-power because the body is representative of the whole cosmos. Literally, the human body is as invisible to the eye of the universe as an atom is invisible to the human eye, yet you are recognised. Your existence is established with the dawn of your consciousness or *pragnya*. The more you evolve through consciousness, the more fear and ignorance dissolve. As you brighten up your being, doubts and shadows disappear.

No university or training institution can teach you how to explore your consciousness. You, alone, must make a sincere, individual effort to expand your consciousness or deepen your awareness. For that you need inspiration. You need a reflection of your being and the guidance of spiritually experienced teachers. Otherwise you tend to forget that you are a powerful being with conscious awareness.

When you walk into a huge crowd, you become small. You are lost because you cannot maintain your own space. You cannot exercise your own thoughts because of the bombardment of everyone else's thoughts. When you are alone, however, you feel your true presence. You can experience, or connect to, the infinite power of the cosmos, and you also become infinite. In the atmosphere of quietness and solitude, you can experience your presence in many places and in many ways.

6
Positivity and Negativity ~ The Dual Unfoldment of the Cosmic Seed

> *The universe itself is a mystic hologram. For scientists, it is a spacious university. For poets, it is a sphere of beauty, imagination and creativity. For artists, it is an enchanting gallery, and for philosophers, the universe is an endless source of rationality and hypothesis.*

The cosmos is primarily viewed from two tangible standpoints; one is positivity and the other is negativity. The human consciousness seems to be inexhaustible in its power, because it discriminates between matter and energy, positivity and negativity, and identifies itself as consciousness through the body and the mind. It soars above all physical constraints to embrace its origin, which may be called super-cosmic consciousness.

The cosmic, conscious seed of oneness divided itself into a twofold existence. This twofold existence became a duality, and yet the common, cosmic connection between them was retained. Then they collided in different times, in different spaces and in different proportions, forming unimaginably vast, beautiful universes.

In the course of this cosmic expansion, the cosmic consciousness, like a tree hidden in a seed, sprouted and spread itself in all directions. The galaxy where we live is one of the infinite branches of the tree of cosmic consciousness.

All that can be seen of it is the frozen part of the cosmic consciousness; the rest is non-corporeal, but can be felt. After a great length of time, man gradually came into awareness and called himself a human being. He named the planet he lived on Earth, and he also gave names to other species.

Dual forces play an equal role in making the conscious and unconscious entities tangible and intangible. Early human beings philosophically viewed these forces as positive and negative. These two forces are the two faces of the same cosmic wave. Negativity is the name of darkness. Positivity is the name of light. Something can be defined or understood as negative only when there is positivity. Positivity can be discerned only in the presence of negativity. Positivity is conducive to one's existence. Negativity is a destructive force in nature and causes one's downfall, but both are essential in order to keep the universe and its beings in perfect balance and motion.

The positive and negative forces also manifested themselves in both hemispheres of the human brain. These two forces exchange and interchange within the body, from the head to the toes. When observed on a smaller scale, the conversion of positive and negative forces is rapid, like the pulses of particles, heartbeats, the life span of micro-beings and the rotation of the earth.

When you observe the motion and conversion of these forces on a larger scale, like the earth's orbit around the sun, the lifespan of the sun, the lifespan of stars and the expansion of galaxies, it appears to be relatively slow and gradual because of our distant perspective. It may take eons of time for dark matter to become transformed into light and for sources of light to lose their light-energy.

When you are filled with energy, you are positive. When you are depleted of energy, you are negative. Even in every atom, the role of these forces can be understood clearly. Whether a person surrenders to death willingly or unwillingly, death has its own significance in the reshuffling and replacement of everything in the universe. Positive nature dwells in the heart, negative nature in the mind. The mind is generally negative, hence it has a strong tendency to question and doubt. Unlike the heart, the mind is a stubborn sceptic. In contrast, the heart is the centre of your being, and is always of a positive nature.

But it is also important, through spiritual understanding and experience, to retain consciousness after departing from the physical body; otherwise one's consciousness may become attracted by the dark side of the universe, like objects sucked into black holes in space. Even a ray of light does not escape the gravitational pull of a black hole. Similarly, when people are negative, or move in a negative direction, this indicates that they are under the influence of the black force in nature, and are heading towards a predicament. *Spiritual awareness is an armour with which one can shield, retain and expand one's consciousness.*

In enlightenment, consciousness spreads to an infinite point and returns in a flash to one's heart. Following that, our consciousness cannot be overpowered by dark matter – the opposite of light and the other side of super-consciousness. Consciousness itself is beyond positivity and negativity, since it is innocent. It is only after descending into this physical vessel, the body, that we achieve our discriminative power of discerning between right and wrong, good and bad, and light and darkness.

As you progress spiritually, you expand your consciousness. As you expand your consciousness, you overcome fear, grief, sorrow and confusion. Each time you gain some experience, each time you receive inspiration, from whatever source, you confirm your growth and expansion. Spiritual awakening is a great and effective change that occurs silently within you. In the material world, any progress you make is subject to fluctuation, since progress in the material world is dependent on countless factors dominated by the mind, desire, need and the availability of resources.

If you achieve something outstanding in sports or any other field, someone might break your record and surpass you, whereas whatever progress you make in spirituality is a concrete accomplishment that will always benefit you. It will never be lost. Any further expansion is left to your individual exertion and endeavour, but progress already achieved remains intact. Materialism is like a rope used to cross from one point to another, or even to another dimension, and everyone is in transit. If you put the weight of your existence wholly on the rope of materialism, you are vulnerable to falling.

People who have been initiated into a cult rarely exercise or regain their freedom. They lose their individuality. Similarly, when one slips into the depths of materialism, it is difficult to regain one's freedom from the shackles of the world. It is an egoistic attitude of the mind that makes us think, '"I" means only the body, or the mind itself, or both, where deeper consciousness is left unrecognised.' One's true and original Self dwells in the heart.

In meditation, thinking usually becomes intense as a result of efforts to control the mind forcefully. Some even make an abortive attempt to stop the mind from being active. People whose meditations are restricted solely to their minds are generally disturbed.

Negativity is the smoke of the mind. Negative qualities are experienced by those who live only in their minds. Such people have no idea what positivity is, and cannot build a bridge between heart and mind. They live like a flower without fragrance.

Those who are spiritual, or those who wish to become spiritual, can experience serenity and a state of equilibrium inside. When positivity and negativity are finely balanced within, you neither laugh boisterously nor cry uncontrollably. You experience immeasurable love and peace. It is not possible to achieve this through usual meditation, which is practised solely within the confines of the mind.

One may be mentally awake and alert, but the spirit in one's heart may be fast asleep. You become receptive when you consciously descend, through your own endeavour, deep into the heart. There, intuition is your guide. You recall and understand the meaning of life and the language of cosmic communication.

When you are positive, you will not experience negativity. Even if negativity enters your boundary, it will be converted into positivity. You may be tossed about by the waves of various circumstances in the mundane world, but internally you are silent – you have learned the art of swimming, and you have no complaints about anything or anyone. You swim gracefully like a fish, and enjoy the water, whether the tide is high or low.

Those who say, 'I don't care' are self-centred and not interested in the well-being of others. An 'I don't care' attitude is an unwillingness to be empathetic and compassionate with others. This does not respect the laws of the cosmos. The 'don't,' which separates the 'I' from the 'care,' becomes a wall. With this attitude there can be no communication, no transmission of thoughts or energies, and no free movement. One day these same people will be on the receiving end of this attitude from others. For them, attraction departs, repulsion sets in, and friendship declines. This is similar to, 'I hate it.' When a person hates someone, this means that first one must hate oneself. This attitude causes enormous damage to the body and mind, sometimes leaving behind long-term negative effects. In hating another, one sends out negative thoughts and vibrations, and in effect, the sender is the first victim.

While you are in a meditative state of consciousness, you overcome negativity and gain inexplicably wonderful and uplifting experiences. Profound inner experiences cannot be handled or registered by neurones in the cortex, since neurones are trained to receive information that generally comes through the senses. When you are deeply absorbed within, fathoming the mysteries of your own nature and life, experiences occur directly in the heart, through the consciousness. This seems incomprehensible when you analyse it scientifically and interpret it rationally, but when you experience this spiritually, you know its truth beyond a doubt. When you experience this spiritually, it becomes an unalterable, concrete truth. Thereafter, you do not need any certification or testimonials to support this experience, because you know it. It is your personal experience.

Positivity. Just one step is enough. With positivity, all sub-positive forces that exist, not only within the atmosphere of the earth but elsewhere, rush to assist the truth-seeker. The same effect occurs when one becomes negative. All negative forces rush in to make one's mind and body the abode for all kinds of maleficent and destructive qualities. But, conversely, when you extend your hands and heart to serve another, you find others who are ready to extend their whole-hearted support to you. Cosmic forces act in the same way. Whatever is seen in the micro-cosmic world can also be seen on a macro-cosmic scale.

Positive people serve humanity and carry all types of emotions. They experience the totality of life. They expand day by day, consciously and spiritually, because the heart has assumed supremacy. Feelings hidden in the mind are susceptible to discovery by hypnosis and other means, but whatever is in your heart is private and safe. When the mind cannot decide, the heart always knows. That is positivity. When you really love someone, you always cherish that person in your heart and not in your mind.

When you think of your favourite dish, your mouth waters and your appetite increases. When you think of a horrible incident, it brings some fear. This may be in a subtle form, but there is fear. So also, the more one thinks of negativity, the more one drifts from positivity. Therefore, those who are positive should exercise, protect and develop their positive attitude by saying, 'I am good. You are good. Life is good. There is goodness everywhere. Let me imbibe and experience only beauty, truth and love. Let me take the best and leave the rest.' With time, the meaning of this will sink into your deeper mind and then into your heart.

Positive vibrations and energy can be transmitted and received through touch. When you consciously touch your own body with your hands, you feel warmth. Such touching enriches the parts touched – the eyes, chest, feet, etc. – and can even cure physical ailments. Touch confirms one's existence in physical form, and also establishes the harmony and fullness of one's being. The body glows when touch is offered.

Negativity leads nowhere. Positivity leads to an intended destination. The heart dances. Consciousness pervades. The mind settles. The intellect becomes an obedient servant. The senses add more sweetness to the melody.

The space between positivity and negativity is neutral, and becomes the medium for the transition of light and dark forces. It can be called a neutral, or unchanged and unaffected force. The entire creation, and anything that the human mind can imagine, can be compared to or be symbolised by a square. Highest cosmic consciousness, with cosmic conscious laws, can be found at the centre of the square. Positive and negative forces stand diagonally at opposite corners of the square. All entities in this galaxy and elsewhere, gather and gravitate to a third corner. The remaining, fourth corner of the square, is a place or position of neutrality. After an infinite amount of time, all will merge into absolute oneness and repeat the cosmic play in an entirely different – or possibly the same – way as we see in the universe today.

Part Two
The Emotional Self

Just as the snake slithers, the lion roars, the nightingale sings and the peacock dances, human beings should show their emotions.

☙ ♥ ❧

7
Emotion ~ A Direct Expression of the Heart

> ***All beings on earth live to exercise and express their full potential. When they do, they look beautiful, because they are aligned with their trueness.***

Everything we feel internally must be expressed in some form, and emotions are the principal way that human beings express themselves. There cannot be devotion without emotion. Emotions are natural, and therefore very healthy. You cannot show your emotions artificially. An upsurge of feeling brings tears to your eyes, immobilises your tongue and makes your heart pound. With it, you radiate profound energy and your concentration and focus on a single subject can be intense. At such times, you feel that the depth of your consciousness is deeper than the ocean.

Emotion springs from the inner Self and creates a strong magnetic field. There can be so much power in your emotions that they surge like waves on the sea. You may lose control of your body and mind. You usually speak less, but communicate more meaning. At such times there is also great transformation. Emotions move you, and invite everyone around you to share your deeper feelings. The minds of highly rational people have difficulty expressing deeper emotions because the connection with their own feeling-heart has withered. They live mostly on a mental plane. One must be truly emotional to be spiritual and vice versa.

Emotion is born out of attachment. Material attachment produces negative emotions, such as jealousy, vengeance, malevolence and similar destructive qualities. When things go against your wishes and desires, you become emotional. Emotional attachment to the wholeness of humanity, nature and other beings brings forth positive emotions, including kindness, compassion and other humanitarian qualities. Your inner Self speaks through emotion.

When you do not express your emotions, you lose touch with your own life and aliveness. Rather than being weakened by expressing emotions, you are strengthened, because you exercise everything you have within you in order to bring out your feelings. To be emotional, something has to touch you, and you automatically embrace so much more when you are emotional.

Love is emotion's epicentre. Just as the sun is the focal point from which all planets in this system have their orbits, so also love becomes the central point from which all lands of emotions orbit. A strong spiritual communication is established when you are emotional. You reach a new peak of experience, but cannot always relate your experience to others.

Emotion is not blind. It is knowledgeable. Emotions surge up in you only when you have awareness of your consciousness. If you do not understand something, how can you be emotional? If you are emotional, you are receptive to another's feelings and thoughts and you respond to them. You reciprocate from your heart, rewarding the other person by offering whatever you have. If you cannot offer material possessions, you show your concern emotionally. There is emotional conversation from heart to heart, rather than from mind to mind.

Expressing true emotion is feeling life deeply. So much relief comes from experiencing emotions. Blockages are cleared. Heaviness is lifted, and your heart becomes lighter.

Your eyes sparkle. There is space. It is pure. You accommodate others and show them great consideration. You expand to embrace humanity. Systematic training cannot help you to express emotions. They must emerge naturally. You cannot artificially stimulate your heart to pour something out. Its expression must be sincere.

Superficial conversation cannot bring up real emotion, and casual utterances of 'I love you' do not help to bring emotions out either. Poets go to the depth of their consciousness to bring out real emotion, and they preserve their thoughts through esoteric language. Great artists express their emotions through their work, and those who are emotional understand the inner meaning of such work. Those who spend most of their time merely in thinking, arguing and being egoistic, find it difficult to express and experience their emotions. No matter how much you do, how much love you shower on others, how many methods you use to express your concern, nothing wakes such people up because the door of the mind has rusted shut. Unless they make some basic effort on their own to open that door, no emotion floods either in or out. Only those who have awakened their emotional self can recognise whether or not another has raised their emotional self.

Even new-born babies may have many ailments, and some may undergo extensive surgery. This is often because the mothers did not express deep emotions during pregnancy. They may have led very cold, unexpressive lives, and hence, gave birth to unhealthy babies.

We cannot become emotional every day. It is not a mechanical or routine occurrence. It pours out when feelings manifest from within.

8
Love ~ Living the Fullness of Life

When you love someone, you love everything about them. You have no reason to hide anything from them because you trust them wholly. You offer your own life. What more could you give?

You are like a flower and your love is the scent. Whoever walks into your presence inhales the fragrance of love and feels a sense of being uplifted. When they leave you, they remember you and cherish the experiences they had with you. It is a noble service that inspires others. This indicates that your existence has touched many hearts.

By allowing yourself to expand through the experience of love, you gradually forget any previous loneliness. As loneliness is forgotten, you become strong, since there is a reflection of your own conscious image in your beloved. Loneliness, anxiety and fear of the unknown will fade away.

Those who are lonely fear anything unfamiliar. When you are continuously occupied in the experience of love, you have no reason to feel depressed. You do not expect anything, but you accept everything related to your beloved. You become the giver. Your giving is offered in a timeless space. The only condition is for the receiver to be receptive, then there is no limitation to your giving. Day by day, love blossoms endlessly. The flower we see in the tangible world blooms with some limitation, in comparison with the unlimited process of this heart-flower blossoming within you.

Nothing hinders the full force of the flow of your love. This stream of love is superior to the flow of a river. The force of a river may abate, but not the flow of love. There is always sound from a river, whereas the flow of love is silently melodious and rhythmic. No one can see it. Only the experiencer can know its depth. This conscious spiritual love leaves no room for disappointment or misinterpretation.

The experience of such love manifests itself in many forms. Pain is relieved. All negative impressions vanish into thin air. You look fresh – a freshness that comes from within you, not from the outside. The freshness of love is realised when your approach is natural.

Your physical body becomes a vehicle through which you breathe the moments of your life. Joy is the oxygen of your inner consciousness. People who do not breathe and feel this joy or true inner love appear to be weak even though they are physically healthy. They have neither given nor received love, and cannot have a vision of their own life. They work repetitively doing the same thing, like ants building an anthill.

This is all part of the unfolding evolution of creation. After you have experienced true love within yourself, you can feel great transformation in your tone of voice, your way of thinking and your lifestyle. Everything becomes refined. Those who come in contact with you are moved, because they are touched with your magnetic power of love. If their minds are conditioned by set opinions, it may take some time for them to realise the profound effect love has on them.

Realisation and experience of love bring transformation in your expression. Your words carry abundant meaning and energies. The words are dipped in sweetness because they emerge from the heart, rather than from the surface. You make your life very meaningful and you feel deeply contented. Those who have not been awakened by that love experience are affected by worries and anxiety. 'What will happen? Where am I going?' These questions bother them and prevent them from sleeping and from being happy, even in their dreams. A shadow of unfulfilment prevails over their hearts, because they do not let themselves bathe in their own emotions, deeper thoughts and innermost feelings.

So, let us all open our hearts and allow ourselves to wake up the dormant love, thus bringing cheerfulness, freshness, higher wisdom and peace into the world.

9
Love and Lust

All conscious entities need and deserve love, no matter whether one is sceptical, scientific, superstitious, dogmatic, philosophical or spiritual. Love has no contradiction; it is a healthy, driving force. Without the expression of love, life is like a desert.

We often mistake lust and infatuation for love. Sincere lovers must glide over lust and not be trapped, because love is the true destination. The experience of love is forever youthful and blissful.

Love is a force of unity. All species, including humans, can be garlanded with a single thread: love. It is the only conscious force that can unite all of humanity. Whatever one's intellectual capacity, academic knowledge and scientific rationality, the experience of love occurs through metaphysical means and a spiritual approach.

Love is the mother, and truth is the father, of all that exists in the cosmos. Love brings an expansion of consciousness. It is the only incontrovertible experience in the world. It makes any discomfort bearable. However rigid or disciplined your attitude may be, love makes you warm, flexible and obliging. This is the magic of love.

Just as iron melts in fire and eventually becomes liquid and flows, so does a stiff, negative person mellow when love manifests. Love is a fire, but it never burns; it acts as a balm.

Love manifests in every conscious entity, be it a plant, an animal or a human being. Fire glows, but love blows like a breeze to its subject. Love has all the purifying properties of fire, but flames soothingly, purifying one's heart, body and mind.

True love is often established when there is sacrifice. This is a major testing point. Infatuation, passion and lust can be seen as just the nails, hair and perspiration of love. While lust is physical, love is psycho-physical and para-physical. Love is the highest, most positive, most moving experience that one could ever have in life.

'Living' is always associated with the physical body. Yet our physical body is more of a station or a centre that is local, or internal, whereas the inner conscious Self can be both local and non-local, or internal and external. In deeper love experiences, you sometimes expand your consciousness internally and sometimes externally. At some point, both facets of experience merge into a state of enlightened consciousness.

Love and lust exist on two entirely different dimensions. Lust is often a source of confusion and conflict, but there is always clarity and calmness in love. Lust is limited and restricted, whereas the experience of love is abundant, cosmic and beyond ordinary conception. If one indulges oneself in extreme lust, one may gain some pleasure, but one loses energy and peace. In love, energy is circulated, not lost.

When you express love, you are adoring yourself, others and nature. Peace, bliss and happiness arise peripherally. But when one indulges merely in lust, one undergoes the unpleasant effects of possessiveness, jealousy, misapprehension and so forth. Lust harbours all these negative qualities.

Lust makes us greedy and tiresome. In lust, the mind is the boss; the body is the secretary, and their activities appear to be that of a business. Lust swings between the mind and body.

Each time you experience love, existence is heightened because you reach many hearts and minds, and you will be remembered by many. Lust is felt by the nervous system, whereas love is experienced by the inner conscious Self where the heart is the doorway. Love begins from within, is then focused on others and later multiplies endlessly until it pervades without limit. One day you become the lover of all species, the lover of the universe and the lover of everything. But the beginning is in the heart, which is the root of infinite love. The nervous system simply channels this love.

In love there is vision. Love is an experience of timeless value. Once we begin to experience love in our lives, everything in and around us becomes luminous and serene. Focusing on every aspect of life becomes easier. Love makes us universal. There is always a sense of insecurity when lust is embraced, because it is not based on trust. In lust, infatuation and biological appetite become the main features of attraction.

Love is self-sustaining. One does not necessarily have to prove love to one's beloved through material objects, since love is the direct experience of the heart and consciousness. You radiate in all directions with no boundary even if you do not see who is standing in front of you or behind you. You do not judge or discriminate as to who receives it.

Love radiates even without your own knowledge. It is such bliss to feel that profound energy. Unlike a river that flows only in one direction, love is like light which spreads multi-directionally. It is a super-force of gravity in a uniting sense, keeping all beings in perfect balance and harmony. There are many ways to bring out love, including greetings, offerings, words, gestures, listening to others or simply through smiles. It seems that modern man is deprived of love. Many of our actions are performed mechanically, without deeper understanding or experience.

In the true experience of love, there is no fear. You have freedom. The full flow of energy is felt. There is no space for negative forces to enter. Negativity arises only when there is stagnation, which comes from the stillness of one's emotions and receptivity. In love, everything is in circulation and movement. One may maintain one's body in good shape and health, and one may also make an attempt to tame the mind, but if love is not experienced in the true sense, then everything is futile.

One should not expect or solicit love from others; it should come naturally. Lust can be mistaken, but love can never be mistaken. In true love, there are no give-and-take dealings. You just give. One's prime focus must be on giving. You do not have to make any physical attempt to give. Everyone is born with inner love. There exists an inexhaustible source within. You simply allow your consciousness to ripple and send love out. You become so occupied in giving that you do not have time to worry about anything else. The more you give, the more you generate. That is the greatest task you can undertake in your life. After giving love, it may return to you, or it may not return at all. However, giving love unconditionally always protects one from disappointment and frustration. Thus, the giver remains ever joyful.

If one confines love only to the body, then one is subject to emotional extremes like dejection or exhilaration. When true love is experienced, you become totally content. What you usually see in the world is often only a vain attempt to please the senses through pleasure, not a sincere attempt to experience love. This is more about possessing property, money, jewels and even human beings. Even in the expression, 'I love you,' for most there is condition, force or command, and this becomes a self-built prison. That is not love. If you want to experience the highest form of love, you have to close the mind and open the heart. You become highly magnetic and others can feel joy and inspiration when they come into your vicinity. You live in them and they go and transfer that love to others.

When you love your own existence you are naturally going to love others. That leads to Self-realisation, since there is no misery or ignorance within. If there is no sunlight, flowers cannot blossom as they should. So also, if there is no light of inspiration in one's heart, the inner, dormant love can never bloom.

Those who do not experience such profound, deep, inner love are unhappy in their lives and tend to disturb others. They slip into all sorts of bad habits and want to extract joy from whatever source they can. They fail to achieve even that. All they gain is transitory pleasure. In order to sense love energies in others, one first has to identify them in oneself. When people extend their good wishes and friendliness to you, it means you have extended yourself to many hearts. You are extending the dimension of the mystic space within you so as to accommodate others in your life.

After such a true love experience, you can feel a great transformation in the tone of your voice, your style of living, your movements, your actions, your very appearance and your way of thinking. Everything in you becomes universal, spiritual and sweet. Whoever comes in contact with you is touched by the power within, even if their minds are stifled. It may take some time for them to realise it, but gradually it does have a positive effect on them. Let everyone open up their hearts and become aware of this treasure they have within. Then they can transmit the light of love to others so that others too can be transformed. This will bring peace and tranquillity to the world.

If one does not receive or give love, one simply exists, and there is no true experience of one's own presence. Thousands of writers cannot express even a fraction of the experience of love. You can ask for money, food, shelter or some other kind of help, but *you can never ask for love. To experience love, you either have to look into the reservoir of love in your own inner being or be receptive to someone else's love.*

All conscious entities become nuclei or reservoirs of love, and love energy orbits around them. A feeling of love opens up a communication line between two hearts, and the hearts themselves become mirrors, reflecting multiple love-experiences to each other. As the earth has its natural resources, humans too have their own natural, inner resources. Just as one finds minerals and other valuable resources inside the earth, one has to go deep into one's inner being if one wants to experience the wealth of love. We have all come into the world to experience love, but we forget this very first objective of life. We busy ourselves in augmenting our material living. Some people argue, fight and injure others, unaware of the treasures of love in themselves and in those they are in conflict with. Our heart pulsates and vibrates because it is our life-giving link to the conscious spirit.

Life becomes comfortable and very satisfying when true love is felt. It can touch anyone's heart if it is given unconditionally. Love is clean and flows like a waterfall. You do not have to test this water, just trust it and drink it. It is pure and salubrious. In love, you are open and sharing, and you will not run out of this resource. No matter how much people absorb from you, you remain youthful, never growing old internally.

Lust is only a fleeting pleasure. It is just a glimpse of the inner joy. It is not real, whereas love is all-embracing. It has everything you deserve and everything you need. You feel secure and protected.

The seasons may change, the moon may wane, flowers may fade but your love can never be reduced in its vigour or sweetness once the flower of love has blossomed in you. Love is strong and its attraction is powerful. Animals respond to the radiation of love energy. Even plants respond to that love. It makes nature speak to you. It inspires you. Much understanding comes with it. Nothing can shake the confidence of love within you, because love is not constructed on any dogma or utopia, whereas lust is like a house built on sand that may collapse at any time.

Lust withers as youth fades. Those who do not experience cosmic, true love, only run after shadowy objects trying in vain to satisfy their minds. They become depressed, thinking, 'I have everything in the world, yet I feel empty. Something is missing.' Although the main purpose of life is to experience this inner love in everything and in everyone, one forgets. Instead, one substitutes a secondary purpose in life, such as becoming rich, successful and famous. One projects all energies only in that direction, but in the end it cannot bring satisfaction. When love stands first on your list all secondary goals can be gradually accomplished.

Love is spiritual. Lust is on the surface and physical. Before you go deep, touching the surface may be necessary, but that is not the purpose of life. Many are trapped in lust and cannot see beyond it because they may not have received inspiration and guidance to journey further. Lust is always binding, whereas love is liberating and ever-expanding. In lust, your happiness depends on someone else's attitude, destiny and approach, whereas in love, you are humble, but independent, and you emanate the same light wherever you go. This quality of love spills over onto everyone and everything, wherever you stay and wherever you travel.

People around you can feel this. It is abundant. How can you measure it? However you may try, it is as if you are trying to measure the quantity of water in the ocean with a tiny container. No scientist can measure love. No rationalist can analyse it. No scholar can write books on it. The moment you try to capture love with your intellect you lose its sweetness, which can only be experienced. All the beautiful things around us in the world enhance and enrich our experience of love, but you should not touch them with the intention of physically examining or distorting their beauty. Just watch them carefully, drink in their beauty and re-establish your experience of love.

In lust, one plucks a flower, smells it, feels it physically and then scrutinises it, analysing how many petals it has, and many other details. As a researcher, you take it apart layer after layer, put it under a microscope and write a voluminous book about it that can be critical, analytical and at times boring.

In love, when you see a flower, you do not go into a botanical analysis. When you have the grace of love, you simply want to observe the beauty hidden within the flower. You want to go into it and become one with its beauty and charm. You don't want to soil it or analyse it, because your purpose is to experience the beauty and love in the flower. You are fascinated by it, you may just give it a gentle touch. All of this is because the flower is in you. Your consciousness has entered this beautiful entity. There is no difference between you and that entity.

You forget your pain, your worries and your worldly purpose. You dissolve in love. There is no difference between love and you, and trying to separate these two would be like trying to separate a flower from its aroma.

Many people worry, moan, cry and become depressed not merely because of physical pain, discomfort or loss, but because they have not tasted the sweetness of love. Does one have the time to watch the sunrise? Is one grateful enough to thank the air one breathes? The answer usually heard is 'I am busy.' Isn't life vapid when you do not experience this love? These types of questions always simmer in the mind.

People want to remain intellectual. We want to analyse things and dissect animals. We want to experiment on everything we can in order to see what the components and ingredients are. In the course of doing research and experiments, the beauty and serenity on earth are disturbed. We are becoming artificial because we are losing touch with our own heart, and have, for the most part, even forgotten it. We are all here on earth to understand and realise truth, to see and feel beauty and to experience love.

The experience of lust is soon forgotten. Afterwards, you look for something new. You may get into a conflict because someone has possession of an object or person that you would like to be yours. If you experience love even just once in your lifetime, you will not forget it, because it is deeply imprinted within and remembered by the heart. You cannot forget it.

Love is a silent and powerful communication between evolved spirits. No one except the experiencers can know it.

When you become strong spiritually, gaining physical strength becomes peripheral. You do not have to do any exercises to gain this energy in the body. What makes the body move? The mind. What makes the mind move? The vital force. What makes the vital force vibrate? The inner conscious spirit. What makes the inner conscious spirit evolve? Love and inspiration. Love is the only natural cosmic drink for the inner conscious spirit. Love itself is graceful and beautiful. How can one embellish it? It is like a flower. Can you decorate a flower? Do you see how far love is from lust?

Love is calm, mystic and settling. When it is experienced in the heart, you do not crave any other thing in the world. You may try for other things, but if you can't get them, you don't regret it because you have achieved the real purpose of life. No matter how many people tempt you with many things, you say 'I have it.' You say this because you have experienced the highest, so you don't worry about the lowest. The highest is so freeing and enriching that returning to the mere pleasures of the material world no longer attracts you.

Still you manage to live a balanced life and not get too deeply involved in external activities. Your explanations and expressions are only an attempt to bring an image into the mind of the listener who has not yet risen to that level. The physical body becomes the central point and the light of love spreads out from it.

Love must not be mistaken for mercy, kindness, forgiveness, generosity or humanity. These are all the extensions of love. Courage is the heart of love. Love must not remain only a spiritual and an internal, personal experience, but should also be manifested on the physical level. Health, wealth, wisdom and illumination of the Self should be the fruits of love.

10
Courage and Fear

Courage is the name of life; fear is its abuse. These two faces of nature co-exist in all species in varying proportions. When fear dominates, it is the most deadly, life-threatening experience that a human being can ever undergo. During that stage, one becomes vulnerable and unprotected. Courage can be regained and fear subdued only when inner strength is marshalled through philosophical understanding.

Courage is life's true name, and fear is the shadow of death. Fear is a negative expression of the mind, whereas courage shows the strength of the heart. When fear dominates, courage withers, but when courage dawns, fear vanishes. Fear does not further anyone's existence. Progress comes from courage. Courage keeps our nerves strong and maintains and increases our energy in times of need.

Fear weakens our existence. When fear fills the mind, our heart shrinks, our blood races and our spine chills, enervating us and the atmosphere around us. Fear is inner darkness – the winter of the mind. It creates anxiety, stress and disease, and at its worst can cause death.

Courage is uplifting and ever-inspiring. When one is alone for a long time, one can become negative. Whilst among friends and family, there is a feeling of elation because energy, love and positivity are shared. When fear is felt on the edge of your senses, you become alert with an overwhelming urge to employ all your resources to protect yourself. Such fear is like the evening, just before sunset, when the amount of light is proportionate to that of darkness. Similarly, courage and fear are in equal balance within you. Fear for one's life is a deeper fear at the core of one's mind. It is like the evening just after sunset. The mixture of darkness and light is not balanced. There is more darkness than light. In this situation, courage takes a lesser place to fear in one's mind. The deepest level of fear comes from the bottom of the deepest mind in us and is like a nuclear force, which can cause heavy damage.

True courage comes from the heart. To exist in the physical form, a reasonable amount of fear is necessary. This fear is manifested as caution, and acting like a guiding star, enables one to progress in the right direction.

Inability to apply intuition, lack of spiritual understanding and ignorance about the laws of nature are the main causes of fear. The more one tries to suppress these fears, the stronger they become. Their pressure can become intense and explode at any time. Fear is a negative force which, when converted into the positive, can make life energetic and enjoyable. Who is not familiar with their own fear? Every victim knows its heaviness and the unbearable, inner suffering it brings, along with an insidious daily increase in deterioration. Certain harmful bacteria can cause pain and disease in one's body, but fear swallows one's very life. Fear is the harmful bacteria of the mind.

When fear descends from the mind into the heart, the heart throbs without the protection of a shield of courage. The mind is fear's main gateway. Fear overpowers the mind and intellect, the senses, and ultimately one's very physical being. It is like the still darkness in the dead of night. No floodlight can banish such fear. Fear creates a tremendous blockage. One needs a tidal cleansing and awakening force to dispel it.

The human brain is endowed with great potential. Circuits in the brain are incomparably more complex than any known computer. The human brain is the source of all scientific inventions, but it becomes helpless and lifeless when fear takes over. These are the times when we can benefit from the inspiration of someone with a spiritually trained mind, who has positive energy and realised courage. A transformative touch from such a person can bring about awareness, returning courage to the heart, restoring strength in the life force, and allowing one to re-experience consciousness. Then, there is no place for fear to dwell because it becomes clear that there is nothing to worry about. Everything can be philosophised, logically discussed, or spiritually experienced. Even death is treated as a leap to a higher experience of conscious life, and not as a permanent disappearance from the face of the earth. Then there is no darkness, only light – the light of life and of true understanding.

Fear emerges from inside when one is unaccustomed to someone or something. When the unknown becomes known, fear disappears, because there is complete vision and a thorough understanding of one's surroundings, situation and existence. At this point, fear becomes an illusion and not a reality. Courage has risen up and heaved a great sigh of relief. Fear is an illusory trickster of the mind. It uses the mind to damage one's health, wealth and peace.

Fear infiltrates the layers of the mind and becomes an enemy under the guise of friendship. One should exercise, breathe and maintain courage as resolutely as possible, imprinting it in the heart. One cannot take lessons in this. It is a self-taught exercise. Do not expect any manual to guide you or any training course to coach you.

Inspiration becomes the source from which courage is reflected. People usually fear the dark because it is unknown, and therefore unpredictable. They cannot infer or hypothesise what may be hidden in the dark or in the future. If there is a flash of lightning, all objects become visible. So also, a flash of spiritual inspiration can make the unknown known and banish fear. When that inspiration beams into one's being, there is no longer any fear.

When one is fanatically religious, one carries some degree of motivational fear. This fear is not obvious since it is a blind fear hidden beneath the conscious mind. There is no fear when there is spiritual awareness. With courage, consciousness expands and fear dissolves, like snow in the sunshine, leaving no trace of fear in the mind. This can be experienced in deep, inner contemplation. Even an open-minded sceptic can prove this through experimentation. But this must be an intense internal experiment. The residue of such an experiment is a stable and everlasting experience of courage.

When you live only in the mind, you are more vulnerable to the danger of negative influences. When you descend into the recesses of your heart, you find it unsoiled and uninfluenced by troublesome outside forces. Many do research and make experiments on the mind, *but hardly anyone studies our real heart – not the physical heart that pulsates and pumps blood, but the heart that is the seat of our feelings, subtle emotions and supra-sensual experiences.* That is the heart that is to be studied. Let us explore our own hearts and expand the horizons of our perceptions and feelings. Though the heart and the mind are co-existent, the heart is the root. It has subtle and sensitive traces of memory and emotional impressions. The heart has immense intuitive abilities to envision things ahead. It is this 'feeling-heart' that makes the physical heart function.

If you would like to feel your heart, keep your eyes closed so that your energy, mind and everything within you is united, and place your hands on your chest. Your touch is a soothing and healthy caress. There is nothing as curative as your own touch. When you touch, you give great warmth and comfort to your body. *You become a self-resourceful person, free of the fetters of outside entanglements.* When you take a deep, conscious breath, peacefully, you experience the energy, freshness and pulsation of this life force. Even when one wants to establish that one exists in the physical form, one often touches one's chest. This confirms and revives one's courage.

Let fear disappear. Let courage remain within you throughout your life. May you not swerve from the path of your own creation. Descend from the heart to consciousness, because you have already descended from the mind to the heart. To do this, project your consciousness towards the centre of your being. There is no way you can lose your concentration, since there is the experience of your touch on your chest, which is connected with the breath itself. Mystically it is a silent self-study. Your actions, thoughts and words, must be charged with courage. You must remember this label, that you are courage, since that is the name of life. No encyclopaedia or thesaurus has provided this meaning so far. The term courage can be added to the list of synonyms for life, because life is also courage.

11
Misery and Happiness

There are mainly two states of feeling that we are bound to experience during our lifetime. These are happiness and misery ~ the ascent and descent of our life. During the dark days there is a means of minimising or escaping suffering. This process involves a withdrawal and reduction of external involvement and activities, and leads us to re-experience the happiness that is stored within.

All human beings, without any exception, have an innate tendency to live happily. Misery is the opposite of happiness. Though feelings of happiness and misery are inside us, we perceive the source of them as outside us. These sources are interpreted differently by each person according to his or her past experience and present needs. These outside sources have two facets, one visible, the other invisible. The invisible sources of happiness and misery are the circumstances, situations, events and undulations of nature. The visible sources are the things we perceive.

What you see in a mirror is not you. When you stand before a mirror, you see the reflection of your own image, but you are the reality. What you see is only the reflection of the mind in a source external to you. When this outside source is clear and lucid, with no ripples or disturbances, then the mind can similarly experience and understand its own reflection clearly. The outcome of this is happiness or joy, which occurs beneath the mind in the heart, and then gradually spreads throughout the body. When that outside source is not clear, but covered in dust, the mind fails to identify its own being, since the reflection is muddled and distorted. This reflection of the mind seems scary and ugly, giving rise to fear, confusion, decline and misery – the opposite of happiness.

Misery is not experienced in the deeper mind but within the surface mind (first mind), since the mind has no clear or exact message to pass on to the heart. So the mind interprets this as misery and suffers severely. Happiness is the day of the mind, while misery is the night of the mind. Happiness and misery follow the mind, and exist only because the mind exists.

Happiness and misery occupy the mind one way or another and keep the heart fully functioning physically and spiritually. Though the mind is extraordinarily capable of understanding itself and the world, *it has its limitations*. It can only think or experience one thing at a time. When people are happy, they believe that their happiness will remain with them throughout life. However, after a while, misery takes over. When you are at the beginning of a happy experience in life, it usually means you have recently undergone a trauma. Reaching the peak of happiness generally means you could be pushed down into misery at any moment.

The mind is like a fiery ball. Neither happiness nor misery can stay in it for a long time because they are ephemeral in their manifestation. Neither can sustain the full weight of your existence for long. After a while one of these experiences makes way for the other. As long as your eyes are open, you are subjected to the influence of day and night. If you want to avoid their influence, you must blindfold your eyes tightly and stay indoors. Similarly, when the mind's eye is closed, you are unaffected by the influence of happiness and misery. But when it is open, you cannot escape from the effect of happiness and misery unless you know the mystic art of blindfolding it.

Some people make their lives miserable without knowing what happiness and misery are, or the difference between them. Such people simply say they want to be happy, but do not really mean it because they are negative and make no sincere effort. Not only do they make their own lives miserable, they also spoil the beauty and grace of others' lives. They are ignorant because of lack of spiritual awareness and inspiration. In reality, there is no misery or happiness outside us. It is the effect of the reflection in us from the sources outside of us. That source could be a conscious or unconscious entity or even the elements of nature. The effect of happiness and misery works upon a person cyclically. The exact span of time of their effect on a person is individual, relative and mysterious. However, you may call it a shift of mind that automatically affects the body.

Some people make their lives miserable. When they are in the hands of misery, not only do they keep their physical eyes wide open, but also the eye of the mind. Eye-to-eye contact brings a strong influence in any act. Such people not only invite misery into their minds, but also into the deeper layers of their existence. After a while, when misery shifts them into the hands of happiness, they are too tired to enjoy it or even keep their eyes open. In misery, such people keep their eyes wide open; when they switch, they sleep in the hands of happiness, with their eyes consciously sealed. They will not open their eyes even if you beat an African drum. After a while, when their eyes are open, they find they have once again shifted into the hands of misery. Even if, by chance, they keep their eyes open while in the hands of happiness, they would dwell on all the past, bitter experiences that occurred while they were in the hands of misery. These people have a remote possibility of escaping from misery. They do not recognise happiness and are suspicious of it.

A person who has imbibed spirituality keeps his or her eyes wide open and fully focused while in the hands of happiness. Such people absorb deeply and achieve, physically, mentally or spiritually, the pinnacle of happy experiences. When they shift back into the hands of misery, they close their eyes and are little affected by the misery. During this time, positive people devise a plan to overcome misery, and spend their time recalling all the sweet experiences they had while under the sway of happiness. Later, when they want to open their eyes, they are once again in the hands of happiness. Such people will seldom see misery in their lives, since misery for them is always diluted by the sweet experiences of happiness. They will make their lives blissful. They always carry a positive message for others, either silently or verbally, making their lives wonderful, joyful and successful because the essence of success is inner happiness.

If you want to transcend these two states of feeling, you have to keep your eyes closed, regardless of outside temptation or agitation. This closing of the eyes means a complete withdrawal of mental activities. A withdrawal of mental activities means cutting down the expenditure of energy, minimising one's involvement in the outside world and reducing the volume of one's desires. This way, there cannot be much effect from either happiness or misery.

Withdrawing means descending from the mind to the heart. If you do not want to be affected by an unpleasant incident happening before you, you immediately close your eyes and you may even put your hands over them to add further protection. This lessens the effect. When there is misery, one has to close the mind's eye, analyse and contemplate internally the background, circumstances and causes of the misery and determine ways out of it.

When engaged in such a noble task, time passes gracefully. Externally, you may be engaged in other tasks in a physical sense, but, internally, you have withdrawn from everything. Now you become like a drop of oil on water, floating but maintaining your individuality. You are not immersed in the waters, so you can make use of the opportunity to increase your spiritual strength. You exercise your patience while in misery and re-confirm your faith in yourself. Then, after a while, you begin to see sunshine again. Clouds cannot cover the sun forever, just as winter comes to an end sooner or later. Now is the time to experience freedom from misery. In your personal meditative state of understanding and experience, you rise above happiness and misery. Even though what could be perceived as experiences bringing happiness or misery come to you, you remain unperturbed and maintain serenity at the core of your being.

Part Three
Personal Expression

*Go touch the heart. Draw the curtain of your eyes.
Inhale the beauty in nature. Exhale all you want to lose.
Go as deep as you can. When you are natural, you become
everything that belongs to nature.*

൳ ♥ ൳

12
Smile ~ A Sign of Joy

If you smile in front of a mirror, you fall in love with your own self.

If we want to cry, we can cry until the last moment of life. If we want to smile, nothing stops us. When we smile we make our life a celebration. *No light is as bright as your own smile.*

When you smile, you silently invite all others to participate in your joy. When you smile, you look natural. But when you cry, you look artificial because your life is not made for crying.

You lighten up your being when you smile. Your pain vanishes. Questions melt away. *Your consciousness expands as you smile.* Whether others smile or not, you can smile. If you worry about others' sternness, you will join them.

You have many reasons to smile, but you cannot give one justifiable reason for frowning. You become positive when you smile. You inspire others. You make your stay on earth remarkable and joyous.

A smile is the song of your consciousness.

You really look beautiful when you smile. Love and joy are expressed through a heartfelt smile, whereas self-protection is like a mask, and can only attract false and pretentious people rather than natural ones. The more make-up you wear, the weaker you become, and the less your inner confidence and beauty shine through. People who live in towns and cities, spend much of their income on personal grooming products, but this does not impress others. Travel to remote villages. There, the people's simplicity creates an everlasting impression in your heart. Even after returning home from a long journey, you still remember the natural beauty you encountered.

A smile is the reflection of your inner joy.

If you still want to cry for the release of suppressed negative emotions, do so, but not as a continual indulgence. If you offer food to people, they may forget you after a few hours when they feel hungry again. If you give some money to people, they may become much greedier. If you are unable to give them money the next time they ask, they might turn on you. True service to humanity does not stop with the physical action of donating food, clothing or money. Smiling for others can also be a true service, because it quenches the thirst of the heart. *When all kinds of treatment fail, you can heal with your smile*, and be healed by the smile of others because a smile carries warmth, love and good wishes. But most of the time we tend to forget our inborn gifts, such as our smile.

Those who are fanatically religious cannot smile, but those who are spiritual can smile. The first qualification of a spiritually progressed person is his or her smile.

When you smile, you spill your love and light around you like milk. It is a silent and beautiful shield against negativity.

If you wait for tomorrow, you will never smile. If you lay conditions on your smile, it will never happen. Some people wait to smile only after the fulfilment of a particular objective, such as getting a job or buying a new house. In these cases, they are blackmailing or conditioning their own smile, and deceiving themselves in the process.

If you are happy and smiling and not showing a sign of frustration and seriousness, today's psychiatry may categorise you as a mental patient. It demands some set standard of behaviour and reaction to society. If you come within its reach and range, you are deemed to be healthy and normal. Otherwise, you may be misunderstood and even treated medically. Since today's psychiatry is still in its infancy, it has yet to grow and face many challenges to accommodate the myriad patterns of human thinking and living. If your smile is true and from the heart, the magnetism of it can light up people around you with joy and cheer. But your smile must be a confident one, not a hesitant one.

Animals cannot smile, but humans have been bestowed with this great gift of being able to smile. You become a great expressionist when you smile. A millionaire smiles. A poor person smiles. When they smile, we do not see any difference. If they don't smile, we do see a difference because there are different reasons for their seriousness. One is serious because of not being materially successful, while the other is serious with the burden of wealth and its implications. These seriousnesses also have different tones. One person is proud of his achievement and the other is serious about her life. Both have failed in understanding the purpose of life.

Many people waste their time in asking questions like, 'What is the purpose of life?' By repeatedly asking such questions, they forget to experience their purpose in life. When someone says, 'I love you,' a positive human being accepts and acknowledges this, and with a smile, thanks the other. A person who immediately shoots back the question, 'Why do you love me?' becomes negative and dark within, because he or she cannot reflect the light of love. In the course of asking too many questions, people forget their own heart and forget to spare time for experiences.

Every moment is precious. In every moment, new layers of your life unfold. There is surprise after surprise. Many times, when you become silent, you receive answers and *great* experiences. You may not be able to explain or convince others, but you are full and content within yourself. You are spiritually rich and internally satisfied.

You convey much through your smile. You look very attractive when you smile, even if you are a hundred years old. Therapeutic centres and other types of health centres are mushrooming. Millions and millions of dollars are poured into investigating new medicines, yet they are not fully successful. If they could highlight and promote the true nature of a smile, they would solve many problems in the world and save a great many resources.

We are beings who have been created and gifted with the ability to smile. It is the simplest way to express our inner joy. A confident smile can improve our health, develop our personality, deepen our awareness and expand our consciousness.

If you forget your smile, your existence becomes dull and obscure. You must always remember and exercise your smile. It will not harm you if you fail to visit sacred places and forget to read the holy texts, but if you forget your smile, the negative forces in the world will invade you. Your vitality will decrease. Your eyesight will suffer. Glands within the body will fail to function normally. You will lose your appetite and many other related problems will follow.

A silent smile is a great positive expression. Just by offering smiles, you can contribute much to humankind's well-being. Your inner space becomes larger than before. Your message should always begin with your smile. Without a smile, whatever you offer cannot be easily accepted by your friends – but with a smile, it becomes complete. You may bring a huge bunch of flowers, but if you give it without a smile, it is not truly given and cannot be truly received. You may bring one withered flower, but when offered with a smile, the smile adds life to that flower and it will be accepted gratefully. If anyone offers something to you without a smile, think before accepting it. It may cause problems in your life. Accept only those gifts which are offered with a smile and grace.

13
Naturalness and Artificiality

All objects existing throughout space and time appear to be toys for the eternal children of the cosmos to play with. Physical emergence and dissolution seem to be the crest and trough of an eternally moving wave of consciousness in the sea of super-consciousness.

All children are born with innocent beauty; hence they look mystically beautiful. Modern humanity is proud to manufacture plastic fruit, plastic trees, plants, flowers, and similar products, as if trying to compete with nature itself. Although those materials have some artistic value, they do not vibrate energy as natural entities do. You know they are synthetic. Such creations stem from the mind, not the heart. When you are close to nature and aligned with the natural laws, you look attractive. Oneness bridges your own physical outline and that of nature. Since there is no difference between the two, losing faith in yourself is the same as losing faith in nature.

Because nature has descended into it, the human body is like a universe in itself, beyond ordinary comprehension. Science is constantly in search of the ultimate understanding of the mechanisms and functions of the body and the complex network of our brain and mind, but it is impossible to fully penetrate the truths and mysteries of nature with the resource of intellect alone. However, if intellect and intuition are combined, then our existence and our relationship with nature can be understood and experienced more effectively.

In this modern age, although life expectancy has increased considerably, health is on the decline. Virtually everyone has some physical complaint throughout the year, which is an indication that humans are drifting away from nature. As we move further away, we become increasingly vulnerable. That is also one of the reasons why certain ailments are incurable. A number of people have regretted undergoing major operations, noticing afterwards an increase in pain and discomfort. Some have even lost their basic health after strong medication. Many times, medical experts overdo treatment for minor physical problems. All such problems stem from a lack of trust in nature.

When you close your eyes consciously, you begin to experience your inner nature. When all your senses are engaged, you are in outer nature. Both are necessary to experience the fullness and energy in one's existence. When you are out with others, usually you become a social being rather than a free individual. You may have certain thoughts about certain people, but you become cautious in your words and actions. Your concern is that others should not get a negative impression about you. This is a refined condition of our society, in which everyone is involved and everyone is responsible.

Often, when you come home, the first thing you do is change your attire for simpler dress. Generally, the next step is to freshen up or perhaps take a shower. You are back home, back to your original nature, back to your heart. Now you don't have to make an impression on anyone because you are not in society anymore. You are at home. Society is out in the street. You have walls at home to keep society out, so you are free.

This is the reverse of how things should really be. When you go out, you must exercise your freedom. When you return home, you are back in a prison. Most people live the reverse. Full freedom is experienced when they walk into their house. As they walk out, society begins casting its influence upon them, so their minds take over and they become different. Their voice changes slightly, their attitude is modified, their way of walking differs. Their name remains the same, but everything else becomes different. They have fallen under the spell of the mind and have forgotten their heart. Their life is manipulated by the mind. Many do not smile naturally. They lose confidence in their personality and beauty. Artificiality is the opposite of nature. When light disappears, only darkness remains. So, also, when naturalness disappears from one's personality, only artificiality is left. You become acutely aware of time, because with the effort that artificiality requires, you cannot play that role for long. Artificiality does have the glamour, or power, of creating an immediate impact on people, and it rules the 'outside' world.

If you connect your consciousness with a bird's, you feel and share that lightness for a brief moment. If you see an elephant, however light your physical body may feel, you feel the elephant's weight in your heart for a fleeting moment, because your consciousness connects in a similar way with the consciousness of the elephant. In this mystical experience the natures of the bird and the elephant are transmitted and reflected back to the original source.

If you think of any object or entity, the inner consciousness is so powerful, your mind immediately connects with it. Even if you can imagine an object or an entity that does not exist on the physical plane, the magical power of nature descends instantaneously and you can breathe in the experience of it. People who are engaged merely in surface mental activities cannot have these deeper experiences, which are essential to expand the horizons of their existence. Most of the time, these experiences come from within.

Nature has two facets. One is loving, the other is savage. Your health, comfort and well-being are wholly dependent on external, natural laws. Nature exists in all conscious entities from a subtle to a gross level. If nature is disturbed, all humans, including any other conscious entities, are also disturbed. If nature were to twitch, there would be massive destruction or other catastrophes on the earth. Such catastrophes include volcanic eruptions, heavy thunder storms, tornadoes, floods, earthquakes and numerous other natural phenomena. Every human is endowed with special abilities to improve, or damage, the health of his or her body or consciousness.

Animals do not make any attempt to impress anyone. They retain their beauty because they are natural. Humans make many attempts to impress one another, but have little to show for it. But when you do not make any artificial attempt to impress anyone, people generally feel comfortable to communicate with you, because the heart has only one language – naturalness, or honesty, which is characteristic of all of human existence.

14
Pride and Vanity

We should become content and appreciative of whatever we have and whatever we get; only then do we become qualified for higher gifts. That is pride. The antithesis of this is vanity.

You sing melodiously when you sing for your own inner satisfaction. But when you want to sing for others, the natural, inner melody may be lost. You dance naturally without any preparation only when you want to dance for relief and realisation. During that moment, dance or song becomes the expression of your heart. The mind becomes the spectator. The heart becomes the guide, not needing an orchestra or audience.

Dance is your true expression. You do not dance for business; you do not dance to win a prize; and you do not dance for applause. Dancing without any ulterior motives is a soulful experience. This is a dance that requires no training or practice. All the elements in you become part of and accompany your dance. It does not matter to you whether the ground is even or uneven, the weather cloudy or windy, or whether there is an audience or not. You feel the urge to dance, and so you dance. Singing is like this as well. Birds sing for themselves because it is their natural expression.

Those who live in vanity cannot sing or dance naturally. Their dancing is strenuous, with every move calculated, because the purpose is only to impress and entertain others. The words 'pride' and 'vanity' are often used synonymously, but they have entirely different meanings. Pride is the first step towards expressing joy. You take pride in your job, which means you enjoy it. It suits your taste and tendency. If you do not take pride in your job or work, it means you are in the wrong job. You feel a sense of pride when you or your loved ones achieve something. You become proud when you are confident in your skills and abilities. Pride gives you a high opinion of yourself and you reflect your inner personality. But if that pride is inflated, it leads to arrogance. Humbled pride is healthy, whereas excessive pride is damaging. Still, to feel the conscious Self, an element of pride is required. When pride is inflated with self-centredness, you bind yourself in your own web. A spider can escape from its web, but the web of over-inflated pride is invisible and many times more complex.

Vanity is pride in its extreme. It is false pride. Unfortunately, artifice and hypocrisy are the very epitome of vanity and the pivot upon which society spins. Vanity is related to what others might think about you. With vanity you are also excessively concerned about the attitude and behaviour of others. Vanity has little logic. You change your dress and mask according to the whims of those around you. You are vulnerable, because your existence becomes shallow.

Vanity is a deep-seated, chronic ailment in the minds of countless people on earth. With it, you take on an alien personality, losing both your individuality and thinking ability. Hypnotised by a narcissistic society, you betray your inner being. You do not listen to your inner voice, but you listen to the gossip of others. You become a puppet through which others play out their own capricious characters. Anything you achieve is superficial, because it is intended only to impress others and is not done for yourself. Any appreciation received this way soon evaporates. You become unsettled in a tide of negativity, losing your inner peace, searching for something that cannot be established logically or analysed intellectually. When others have something, you feel you must have it too. There is no space for Self-inquiry, such as, 'Why do I have to have that?' You sacrifice your values for something that does not bring satisfaction. 'They have it, so I must have it too.'

Pride is an unrefined, positive quality. A touch of pride is necessary to maintain and protect individuality. Expansion of one's consciousness becomes remote while caught in the wind of vanity. Like a flag in the wind, it has no direction of its own; it flutters in whichever direction it is blown. So also, when caught in its web, your existence flutters according to the kind of society around you.

Although love is universal, it is presented according to each individual's capacity and taste. Even the reception of love varies from one individual to another. When you say 'I love you' to someone, they do not necessarily receive it in the same mood as you express it. Levels of emotion vary according to the states of consciousness in people and how much they have evolved. Those who have not evolved, or who are not spiritually awake and who live in vanity, misunderstand and receive the words 'I love you' purely as a physical expression. If you have an open mind, if your pride is subdued, if you are pursuing the truth and if you really want to feel love within you, then you can experience it.

15
Admiration and Flattery

Genuine admiration is inspirational, natural and complimentary. Flattery is short-lived and superficial, and its after-effect is denigrating.

Admiration is natural. It is the expression of sincere, inner feelings and is often conveyed without sophistication. Compliments emerge directly out of one's heart. The mind has no role to play in such heartfelt and innocent appreciation. Admiration can be expressed for another's beauty, quality, achievement and goodness.

In flattery, you deceive both yourself and others. Flattery is a psychological tactic to win someone's favour. It is contrived and pretentious. In flattery, you use your mind but not your heart, because the approach itself is superficial. Your only purpose is to impress someone, to make them do what you want. It is an insincere strategy with an ulterior motive. In flattery you become social and materialistic and limit your space for conscious expansion.

In admiration, there is every opportunity for expansion and growth. It is not easy to admire others. It takes ability to identify the nobility in another person. When you admire someone, you also inspire him or her. Anything said in admiration is true, since it comes from natural feelings. You use your individual style and put your heart into it. Your behaviour is simple and humble. You are not after any gain. You are just offering your admiration because you perceive something admirable in another. You do not first think about whether or not the other is ready to receive your admiration, because your compliments just flow from you instinctively.

Admiration is a selfless action, offered with true enthusiasm. It is a service to humanity. We cannot know how much joy and elation others experience when they receive such admiration. It re-establishes one's true nature and the positive side of one's existence. In admiration, the truth is transmitted in the form of thoughts and energies.

You can admire others only when you are spiritual. People who are not spiritual do not find it easy to admire others. You have to have a big heart to acknowledge another's goodness, growth and progress. In admiration you are above hypocrisy. Once you develop this quality, you expand day by day. You find no pain and no darkness, and you make your home wherever you walk. Admiration offers you a shelter wherever you go. You do not feel you are alone, for you see your reflection in many people. It is one of the ways to experience your consciousness.

Flattery leads us nowhere. When you engage in flattery, you lose your identity, because you re-establish the hypocrisy hidden in you, which is a stain on your personality. Materialists and opportunists use flattery as the usual language of their daily life. They live on a day-to-day basis and frequently fall into depression. People who have been flattered usually realise sooner or later that it was all a false adoration, and they no longer keep a place in their heart for the person who flattered them. In contrast, admiration is profound, inspirational and natural; nothing thwarts your progress when you acquire and exercise such a noble quality.

For anyone receiving your admiration, it is a great celebration, like a festival. Admiration is a spiritual gift you can naturally offer to another. You do not plan it or work at it. The moment you are aware of what you admire, you want to broadcast it. You offer it openly and without hesitation to people. This brings conscious expansion in you and encourages others to progress. You also become true friends. They identify the goodness in you, and you admire what you see naturally in them. You do not need lenses to see the goodness that exists in others. All you need is a keen spiritual eye. Your heart is clean and your mind is silent, because your heart has overpowered the mind. You become the listener of your heart, not the follower of your mind.

In flattery your heart recedes, and your mind mutters. It is so obvious that even a child with some basic awareness can identify an insincere attempt to win its favour. A flatterer creates an illusion of himself or herself and contributes nothing towards the development of humanity. Instead, he or she becomes a virus which others catch. There is selfishness, narrow-mindedness and sheer materialism involved, because the flatterer is spiritually blind. Such people have dry emotions. Any tears they show are merely crocodile tears. They do not mean it. They are insincere.

Admiration, on the other hand, is felt in your heart. As an admirer you will not feel jealous of another's progress. Your conscious spirit is brighter than the full moon. You blossom more than a flower. A flower can only bloom in certain seasons, but you bloom at any time, even without the sun or the moon, in cold or hot weather. You shine with your noble qualities. When you admire someone, with sincerity to the core of your being, it is a rich compliment to them. And you also get a positive reflection back to you – an inspirational response. This is one of the ways you can ascend to higher levels of evolution in your life.

Every admiration you give is a checkpoint on your journey. It strengthens your inner conviction and the depth of your being. When someone admires you, you become all ears and listen to every nuance in that admiration. You feel so grateful, you are ready to offer something in return. The first gift you offer when you receive admiration is 'Thank You'. It is a spontaneous positive response that means you have received the compliment and that it has touched you and revived your inner confidence. The other person is also moved by your response.

Where is flattery? Where is admiration? They are as far apart as the north and south poles.

16
Humility and Arrogance

Arrogance is strong and stern but unartistic. Humility is tender, sustaining and sinuously artistic, like a river.

You can experience the bliss and beauty of life when you have the tenderness of humility. Humility is the primary quality that leads you deep into the spiritual universe. You look appealing when you are humble, appearing both simple and yet great. Humility should not be taken to the extreme; rather it should be a combined expression of humility and modesty. With this quality of humility, you become a good recipient of higher wisdom. You are like a self-illumined heavenly body. You become less affected by hostile forces. There is no shadow of doubt or stiffness in you. You are flexible and flow like a river obeying the earth's gravity. If there is a mountain obstructing you, you flow around its base and slip out of difficulty into ease. The stream of joy in you continues unabated. If any natural disaster befalls you, you simply stoop down for just a brief moment to let it pass, and then you rebound like tall coconut trees on tropical islands after a hurricane. You set a beautiful example for the world in all your actions, which are without noise and ostentation.

You have no selfish motive in any of your goals. You walk like an elephant, with firm, grounded steps. You expend time and energy thoughtfully. You mock nothing and no one, because you are flowing like a river with all humility and tenderness. Even your breath is composed. Gentleness is seen and heard in your every word and action. Everything is natural and normal within you. There is uniformity and a harmonious flow of thoughts. You become a great host. Many people want to be with you to enjoy and share in your humility. They cannot define what it is about you that attracts them, but they feel something deeply in their hearts. You notice this in the expressions on their faces as you leave them. You appreciate your life and you appreciate all the beautiful things that come within your sight, because of your humility. You encourage others without ever projecting yourself on another's screen.

You glow and shine without having to depend on others for your light, because humility is just like the fuel in the sun. The sun does not have to depend on other sources of energy. It has been giving light and warmth since its birth, and will continue to give light and warmth for millions of years to come. So also, you shine so humbly and simply that even people who come near you can feel that tenderness and calmness in you. When you are humble, your heart is moist, your mind is pleasant, your nerve centres experience relaxation, your eyes speak of compassion and your hands radiate such warmth that just touching any cold person is enough to energise them.

This is your *Sadhana*, or spiritual practice. You become super-sensitive to thoughts emitted by others. Your humility brings a permeability that allows light, love, thoughts or any other quality to pass through you, and your existence thus becomes vast and profound. There is a touch of humility in everything you do. Even if you are rewarded and admired by people, you still exercise your humility. Who would not love to build a relationship with you? Anyone would gladly be your friend, because you are like a harbour they can visit safely. You never say 'No.' You give whatever you have, humbly and generously, and the paradox you find in this is totally opposite to what is believed in the mundane world: you remain abundant even though you are giving.

There is little room for conflict and contradiction. When you imbibe humility deeply into your inner being, you are fresh and well-settled. You do not worry about the things that commonly occur in your daily life. You just assimilate them within you. You expand in many ways.

Now let us go to the extreme opposite end of our existence. There you see those who are spiritually blind because of their arrogance. They have blocked their minds, and are rigid and stiff. Such people have lost control of their lives, and rarely feel the sensitivity of the forces in nature. Love experience is always a mirage for them because of their deep-seated arrogance. They cannot find joy anywhere. Wherever they walk, arrogance follows them like their shadow. They have set opinions and cannot see anything special in the universe.

They may hold many credentials. They may have accumulated wealth, but everything may look stagnant and empty because they have a void in their hearts. You can see the arrogance in their very appearance. They frown and wrinkle their faces while speaking. They look decrepit even if they are physically young. Their eyes do not rotate normally because they are stiff-necked. They are disinterested in other people, only aware of their own achievements and their own possessions. Their arrogance does not even allow them to smile when you tell hilarious jokes. If they smile, you can sense that it is a cover for their arrogance, which is a product of ignorance.

Arrogance is not a foundation on which one can build and expand, whereas humility provides a strong ethical, humanistic and spiritual foundation. Such a foundation will continue to exist for future generations. In humility you become spiritually evolved and feel the fulfilment of life. You experience many sides of life in a short time. Just a mild glance at something can leave a lasting image in your mind. Anything you say is sweet and profound. Whatever you do, you do with utmost fidelity, and you reap the benefits with humility. Humility is a lifting force that takes you to heightened states of conscious experiences and a feeling of unity within and without.

17
Humour and Seriousness

In order to make life meaningful, one has to experience both humour and seriousness in life. Humour eases tension, relieves pain, improves health, energises the body and brings relaxation to the mind.

Humour created by mocking others, making fun of people in a contemptible manner, unnecessarily provoking others and causing tears and enmity, is not healthy for anyone. In extreme cases it might result in a permanent rift and separation.

Humour that is extracted out of constructive criticism, direct teasing, friendly imitation or any other positive means results in strengthened friendship, an improvement of knowledge, growth of personality and an expanded state of awareness.

Seriousness is as important as humour. Seriousness born out of self-centredness, pride, egoism or a superiority complex is not inspiring, either to oneself or to others. Seriousness that implies one's responsibility and concern creates a positive mood and attitude in a person.

The universe is going from order to disorder and again from disorder to order, in a wavelike motion. All species form the organs of life of the universe, and are driven to undergo this irrefutable law. The inexorable motion and growth of the universe is irreversible. Human beings, in particular, have accepted this and tuned their minds and consciousness to the law of orderliness. When this orderliness of life is reversed, it momentarily looks ugly and ridiculous. This abrupt and spontaneous reaction triggers an emotional response, and is expressed by giggling, expelling air rapidly through the mouth or by laughing boisterously. It is a sudden and involuntary expression. It happens in an instant. One cannot even think when one is impelled to behave in such a manner. It is an enigma, called humour.

Humour can be playful or mischievous, going from order to disorder in the inevitable evolution of the universe. It is like energy, or matter, that descends, deteriorates or breaks apart, moving from one form of order to the other. Conscious entities have difficulty accepting the sudden, distorted move from order to disorder, hence there is a noticeable, immediate biochemical response, which may be noisy or silent. When burglars break into a house there is nothing strange or funny about it. It is the way one expects things to be. However, when burglars break into a police station and rob it of its valuables, that brings humour.

Similarly, it is natural for a dog to bite a person when it is irritated. However, when a person bites a dog, that is unexpected and gives rise to humour. But humour is short-lived, like a bubble in water. While engaged in humour one becomes an extrovert. Everything is focused outside. One's own identity is totally forgotten at such times. Everything is projected outside. One is lost in grasping the image of the humorous situation and responding to it. Sometimes, in prolonged humour, your personal dignity may become affected, and your personality may become shallow. You are not aware of your actions, behaviour or even of the consequences of your attitude.

When you imitate someone with the sole purpose of denigrating his or her personality, that can give rise to humour. If you make another a fool, that can also make one laugh. You observe that kind of humour in everyday life. When a person slips on a banana peel, others usually laugh at him. Rather than rushing to help him, they enjoy a good laugh. The person who is subjected to that humour is affected. He can lose his temper and shout, or if he has some pride, he may bear the pain and humiliation alone or seek outside assistance. You cannot see even the subtlest humorous mood on his face after he has undergone an experience like this. The fall was a slip from order to disorder, happening rapidly and unexpectedly. The disorder once again comes into order. He will be more cautious in the future.

When humour ends, one enters seriousness. Humour is short lived, whereas seriousness is long lasting. Seriousness is a way of life. It exists from arrival to departure. Birth occurs with seriousness. The mother is serious. A new-born baby, as a fresh entrant into the world, is serious. People who know obstetrics are also serious. When disorder manifests, jumping the methodical pattern of the universe, the child becomes sick and serious. The conclusion of life is also serious. That is your true face.

When you are serious, you are concerned about your well-being. You become an introvert and a deep contemplator. You have a thorough understanding of your responsibilities, of the situation and of your existence. If this seriousness is followed by solitude, it can be significant, meaningful and effective. You display a tremendous amount of concentration when serious. You are alert. You feel a column of energy from the top of the head to your toes. There is absolute oneness when you are serious. You are attentive internally and externally. You can go to someone's rescue. You can avert danger. You can better perceive and assimilate information, or stimulation, coming from the outside atmosphere. At times, seriousness enriches your personality and dignity. It creates a mystic atmosphere around you. An invisible force surrounds you. You are serious. This seriousness is not a negative seriousness.

Sincerity is the spine of seriousness, and silence is its voice. When serious, you speak less, but convey much more. Everything in you is fully controlled. All types of emotions are completely held in balance.

Humour cannot embrace all of the subtleties of one's feelings, thoughts and emotions, since humour itself is trivial and fleeting. Unlike humour, seriousness is profound and mystic.

Seriousness alone can solve problems or crises. Humour cannot solve them. When you have discomfort or difficulty, in body or mind, you ought to be serious. Seriousness looks stiff and stern, and seems unapproachable, but it can go deep and bring out the required energy currents, bliss, intuition or creative ability to smooth your path to healing and fulfilment. When seriousness is maintained, humour just passes without disturbing your identity and existence. You will not be affected or influenced by negative humour. You stay sedate and continue to remain serious.

Seriousness is also like a submarine. Just as a submarine takes you under the surface of the sea, so also the submarine of seriousness takes you under the surface of your consciousness, where you kiss bliss and float up with its joy. It is a positive joy, not only experienced by yourself, but also diffused like light to all who surround you.

Seriousness is also like a shield. It guards you against negative outside influences, including thought waves or other affecting factors. Internally, you are serious; externally, others do not need to recognise your seriousness. Your seriousness is only to extend your journey of life comfortably, with care and protection.

Humour is like refreshment. It is refreshment only for the mind. You should smell and breathe it out, not storing that breathe which endangers your health and peace. If we allow humour to control us, then all life would be humorous. One day we would realise that life is not experienced in the right direction, or to its fullest degree. Such humour can be negative, so the benefit of spiritual seriousness is emphasised. It can be an uplifting force. It is so strong that it can create a unified field of consciousness within and without.

When you have to face something, you do not make jokes. You take it seriously. And, when you take it seriously, that means you are careful, competent and courageous. You will certainly overcome many obstacles, because of your seriousness. You don't play pranks and frolic, but you play the role of your life with acceptance, grace, vision and conviction.

There are many comedy movies. Few of them have been appreciated or universally recognised. Most great films and plays are tragic, because of their seriousness. Seriousness is the face of one's consciousness. This is not a blind or rigid seriousness, but seriousness with weight, quality, dignity, humility, sweetness and concern. It is an inspired seriousness, which is far from humour.

A monkey's very appearance and whimsicality are humorous, while the lion is the epitome of seriousness. A river, stream or a rivulet may make a little noise, whereas the ocean is magnanimous and serious. You can hear the sound of its waves from the distance.

When you are in humour, you are just on the surface of living. In seriousness, you reach the summit of life. You can see the panorama of your life. You feel as though you are reaching out to the skies. You also feel the earth beneath your feet, delicately and sensibly. Every step you take is firm because of your seriousness. This kind of seriousness is necessary for one's spiritual expansion. You are not lost in humour, but rather enlightened in seriousness.

Conscious seriousness increases the power of the will.

18
Gratitude ~ Pathway to Bliss and Realisation

We usually remember people who have caused trouble for us. We even ruminate over the same past, unpleasant events again and again, however pleasant the present moment may be. We would be better off to recall all the people and forces that have assisted and supported us.

Even if the present moment is miserable, make it a happy event by remembering all that we have to be grateful for. This leads one to celebrate life.

When you really want to express gratitude to someone, you cannot do it pretentiously. Gratitude is a very special human quality and one of the stairways to realisation of the conscious Self. When someone tries to express gratitude to ingratiate themselves with others, or to gain something, it is noticeably awkward and cannot truly succeed. Children are especially aware when gratitude is expressed insincerely, and they turn away from those who do so.

You enter an exceptional state of joy when gratitude is expressed truly. Just as seeds sprout, gratitude is expressed from the heart to offer your true appreciation, without the use of any strategy or tactics.

The expression of gratitude establishes your spiritual existence while you are living in a physical form. You rarely forget anyone or any source that may have helped you. True gratitude is expressed not through the mind, but through the heart, using few words and conveying a great deal. This is genuine expression. There is no ulterior motive, except to show what you have felt deeply within. You use your own language, your own style and your own method to express that gratitude. If you have nothing to offer, you look for natural things such as flowers, fruit or even a stone to express how you feel, and you infuse abundant meaning, emotion and thankfulness into these gifts.

When you express gratitude, you also express humility and beauty. You use all your energies, inner resources, stored thoughts, feelings and concerns to complete the expression of gratitude. You do not observe any formalities. At such times, you drink in humanity. The true expression of gratitude has no intention of winning anyone's favour. You express it for your own self, innocently and naturally. You acknowledge by its feeling that you have received inspiration and support from many people in the world, and that no one's life is independent of others.

Life is like a novel. No novel has just one character. Some characters are good, some are bad and some are neutral – the possibilities for the plot are endless. Similarly, your own life involves many people and many different circumstances. It is never abstract or absolutely independent of the support, good wishes and inspiration of others. *Your happiness actually lies in the happiness of others, and your prosperity often lies in their progress and well-being.*

Other people's happiness is contagious, and they naturally influence you. Likewise, when someone close to you is in difficulty, how can you fully celebrate your own happiness? Each of our lives is very complex, full of intricacies and mazes, and is inextricably interwoven with the lives of many others. No novel, epic or legend could equal our own voluminous story. If one were to record unremittingly all the events, from minor to major, that occur in one's life, all the libraries in the world would be filled with a single person's story.

Imagine how immense and complex your own story is. Even on the mental level, a huge brain would be required to thoroughly remember all the events of your life. Fortunately, you remember only a few moments, some main events and important things in your life. It is an enigma that although you do not have full control of all the happenings in your life story, you are its main character. You make your story inspiring and fascinating when you express noble qualities such as gratitude.

When you express gratitude directly and unassumingly, you create a golden atmosphere both within yourself and within those to whom you offer your gratitude, and you become an example for others. Not everyone can express gratitude. Many cannot even express it to their own parents, family members or friends. Materialists feel that something will be lost if they express gratitude. They float on the surface of joy called pleasure. Such people neither appreciate their own lives nor do they acknowledge others from whom they have benefited. True joy does not come from material things.

Gratitude is a spiritual expression from the heart and brings great blessings, even if the recipient is not ready or willing to receive it. Complimenting someone else and the good they have done brings growth and expansion to the person feeling grateful. Gratitude is like a tree, growing and branching out, bringing benefit to itself and others. The tree of gratitude leads one to the height of life.

Physical light helps identify things in the outside world, but there is also a light within that helps identify our priorities and the direction of our life. We exist consciously and physically, since we are the combination of the visible universe and the invisible forces. We are also the representative of the light of life. It can also be called a mystic light. Greed, lust and other negative qualities can adversely affect this light. Ingratitude is another of the elements that can make this inner light flicker, fade and even fail.

Lack of gratitude is a major deterrent for the emerging personality, whereas the force of gratitude comforts one in every aspect of life, aiding ethical, social and spiritual coherence. It takes us further in realising our life purpose. Expression of gratitude is a sign of one's worthiness for further growth on both physical and spiritual levels. It inspires the person who is appreciating, as well as the one who is being appreciated.

19
Respect ~ The Gesture of a True Human Being

Respect reflects back to us from others only if we have respect for them. We cannot expect others to respect us when we do not have respect ourselves.

Inspiration, love, fortune and respect have to come on their own. You cannot achieve them forcefully. They are not objects that can be grabbed. You cannot make any mechanical effort to receive respect, because it is out of your hands. Someone else has to offer you respect. That is his or her decision. You may wish in your heart to be respected, but you cannot force it to happen. If people do not show you respect, you should analyse your attitudes, the motives of your actions and your behaviour. Has self-centredness or selfishness consciously or unconsciously manifested? There must be a reason – sometimes hidden – for this lack of respect. Perhaps you mistrust yourself, or you may have developed a pessimistic attitude towards your presence. In this case, a trace of disrespectfulness about yourself is sensed by others and, not being able to understand you deeply, they reflect back what you give out.

Respect is not a business commodity or a legal obligation. It has to be given and received naturally. You cannot give respect artificially, as if it were a material object to be cast out with the words, 'Take it!' Respect has to emerge from within.

You do not lose anything when you respect others. On the contrary, you benefit greatly. Your emotional level becomes balanced when you show respect to others, and this can be done in many ways. There is no school that teaches exactly how to respect others. Respect is a human quality that should come from within, naturally. It is a preliminary stage to love. Feeling and experiencing respect within yourself, for your heart, mind and body, qualifies you to experience love.

Whatever you perform selflessly or altruistically is never done in vain. All thoughts, deeds, actions and their consequences are observed and stored in the heart of nature. They reflect back on the person with love. It is only we who compartmentalise our actions into good and bad. Many a time we are biased and limited in analysing our own actions and their consequences. But the higher nature has its own broader outlook on human consciousness. You can truly express yourself only when you do not have expectations from the outside world. If you expect something in return, then your action really becomes a transaction, even if it is in the guise of humanitarian or spiritual effort. True giving is done without calculation. When you give respect, there is nothing that can be seen, but the receiver will definitely feel something. You have your own reasons for respecting that person. When you give respect to another, it means you have stored a good image of them and you never feel anything against them. You are always positive about those whom you respect.

Respecting others gives you a shower of grace. You want to encompass all that comes within your view. You don't ask for respect but rather you show it and give it, and it is received. Just as you feel uplifted and happy when you receive respect from someone, so also the person who receives respect from you, feels elated and exhilarated. The heart leaps with joy.

On the other hand, when disrespect is shown to others, notice how much they suffer. Pain and discomfort that arise out of disrespect may be more severe than physical pain.

Disrespecting another means you do not have the slightest feeling of positivity towards that person. It destroys any relationship, making it very difficult to rebuild. This brings loss from every angle and offers no hope of expansion. No matter if the other person is a child, a young girl or an old man, all beings deserve respect.

By giving respect, you establish your greatness as a human being. It is a noble quality. What the other receives cannot compare to the amount of your inner happiness and satisfaction. *This* is true giving. Even giving your wealth will not bring as much happiness. Respect that is shown to you is remembered throughout your life. You may not be able to understand this today, but you surely will in the future. You do not go from door to door to show your respect, but you show it especially to those who come within your sight and within your conscious periphery. Respect adds meaning to your life. It is an indestructible and metaphysical gift that you offer to others.

The same energy that is expended in criticising others can be used to the same degree to respect others. In this way, the experience of inner love becomes inevitable and flows freely. Respecting yourself also means you have confidence in your own qualities.

Whether or not the other receives it, you give respect. You do not become disappointed if they don't receive it – you simply give it. After receiving your respect in whatever way you chose to express it, the eyes of those who are sensitive and receptive will reflect their inner happiness.

When you offer respect, it comes back to you. It may not come back today or even tomorrow, but it will certainly come at some point later in your lifetime. Even if you do not enjoy the respect that reflects back to you, your family will. Nothing is wasted in the universe. Everything is accounted for. Each particle in the cosmos has some significant role to play and no particle collides meaninglessly with any other particle. Each has some task to perform.

We always look for an immediate response – 'I helped this man. Why isn't he helping me?' Even before offering help, we may calculate to see how much we can get back in return. That is not true service. You not only lose in such a transaction and communication but it also brings disappointment and dejection. However, when something is offered without expectation, at the very least it gives internal satisfaction, and you say to yourself, 'I have done this sincerely.' You know that. Others may say that you have not given respect and love to your family members or to your friends, but deep inside you know you are sincere and honest and that you gave it unconditionally. Your heart is open, your conscience is clear and you sleep well. You can face anyone courageously.

A great advantage of respecting others is that it brings all these qualities to the giver. So, give respect. If you give and give in the material world, you might become poor, but the more you give in the spiritual world, the richer you become. Such giving is always generated from within you. It is the unique gift of your birthright. Giving respect is a noble quality that leads one to Self-realisation.

Part Four
The Quest

Finding an answer is not the end of your quest, it is the beginning of a long, labyrinthine journey.

20
Question and Inquiry

Most people spend their whole lives asking questions of themselves and others. They are neither happy nor satisfied, even after obtaining some answers. The question 'Why?' makes you tired and seldom comforts you. It is true that one cannot gain knowledge without asking questions, but one has to stop questioning at some point. There is a stage at which you ought to enter silence. Keep questions only in the mind, never bringing them into the heart. Only then can peace, love, happiness and realisation of the Self become possible. You gain scientific understanding by asking questions, but with inner growth and in the spiritual dimension, you enfold questions into the single powerful question, 'Who am I?' This question is posed within, silently and sincerely, not in an interrogative manner but in a positive mood. This is the beginning of inquiry, and will eventually result in the complete awakening of your dormant vision, wisdom and energies.

When you ask a question you become an extrovert. A question arising in the mind can be asked in two ways, internally or verbally. A question builds in the mind and when it is mature, it finally explodes. A question cannot arise without having some rudimentary information as its basis. Questioning takes energy, and a question will bother you continuously day and night until you offer it nourishment in the form of an answer. When you question, you get answers relative to the type of questions you ask. Some answers are satisfactory but others may not be. Finding an answer is not the end of your quest. It is the beginning of a long, labyrinthine journey.

Questions multiply endlessly, like bacteria. When you reach the ninety-ninth question, you will have forgotten the first one. You can keep yourself so busy asking questions, that you have no time to relax, to greet your friends and family or even to smile, because your mind and lips are occupied in weaving questions merely to quench the curiosity of your mind.

Those who have trained themselves only in asking questions look drained of energy. As you move on in this way, you may also become negative, because you neither experience joy nor do you allow others to be joyful. Questioning is noisy and chaotic and usually contentious, whereas inquiry is deep, internal and silent. Inquiry brings experience, not answers. The end of questioning is the beginning of inquiry. With inquiry, you have profound experiences, eventually leading to enlightenment. You may not be able to convince others of what you have experienced, but you are filled with inner certainty. Asking questions is not your inner nature; it is the nature of your mind.

When you have physical discomfort, you go to a doctor and ask him or her questions about it. You usually accept the answers you receive, as you know little about physiology. Even if the answers do not satisfy you, you usually follow the doctor's recommendations without further investigation, since your goal is to find immediate relief. This can be temporarily acceptable, but when questions arise concerning your emotions, your feelings and your personal experience of the body, mind and spirit, where can you go to ask them? You might go to a psychologist to ask about your mental health. He or she would give you answers that are often subjective and clinical, and you might return home without satisfaction and probably with more confusion.

'Who am I?' is an inquiry. 'How do I look?' is a question. 'Who am I?' remains until you are inspired. After a time, through spiritual practice, understanding and experience, 'Who' melts away. 'I am' remains, like a mountain after its cover of snow melts in the summer. This will help you to escape from the grip of material fetters and Maya. The moment you embrace 'I am,' your progress is certain and enlightenment becomes possible. 'I am' remains unalterable. It is you. You may lose your hair; your face may sag with age; the features of your body may change; but 'I am' remains constant.

'I am' is the pivot of your conscious Self. It keeps you young and energetic throughout your life. You may have lost your external resources, but you can reconstruct your future because you are positive. 'I am' is absolutely positive. It can never be shaken, for it is based on experience rather than on information received from the outside world. 'I am' existed in the past. 'I am' is in the present. 'I am' will remain in the future. At any time the experience of 'I am' can flash like brilliant lightning.

I urge you to become inquirers if you are determined to experience and realise the spiritual dimension of your existence. It is a realisation that cannot possibly come simply from obtaining degrees at universities or from reading books. When you become self-aware, you find that the answer to any question becomes available to you silently and mystically. It is only the intellect that bubbles on the surface of the mind, generating question after question, whereas intuition unfolds when you become an inquirer.

21
Clarity and Confusion

Living outside ourselves is extremely hard, and when we are habituated to this, it seems immensely difficult to get into our own inner being. But, with practice you become familiar, once again, with the way into your own home. You begin to be the master of your own home.

We achieve clarity only when we devote our time to some meaningful activity. We achieve clarity when we confidently perform some action.

Confusion is a blockade that sprouts inside us. For this there is no medicine. There is no treatment or healer who can take confusion out of us. Confusion worries and drains us, distancing us from our purpose in life.

The spirit dwells inside, and while confusion drains our energy, the mind wanders outside. Thus we remain unsettled, like vagabonds. Until confusion melts away, there can be no harmony within. We lose our power of receptivity and our ability to grasp anything. Since there is no inner fulfilment or contentment, everything is in utter disorder within us and we reject everything. We feel chaos, disorder and commotion internally.

Those who are impatient suffer from confusion. Those who have a lot of desires or are too materialistic suffer from confusion. Those who have too many expectations also suffer from confusion. Confusion is a disease of the mind. Confusion is not healthy. Everything looks foggy and dull. Confusion is the mist of the mind. Eye specialists may certify your vision to be acute and sharp, but you still cannot see your own path, because it is obscured by confusion. You cannot read or write. You cannot think or express yourself. Everything is in such disorder, that you don't even realise you are confused.

Your concentration is dissipated and your memory is in disorder. When you want to remember a person, someone else comes to mind. When you do not want to remember a person, the thought of him or her bothers you day and night. In such a state, you just do what seems absolutely necessary.

Insecurity also causes confusion, fear and anxiety. Those who suffer from it can easily be noticed. They have an unsettled appearance. Their eyes do not focus properly. Their minds are not in accord with their senses, and do not accept the messages received through them. Both the mind and the senses will lose their connection with the inner conscious spirit.

We are all the quanta of the brilliant cosmic light rays.

When we are overpowered by our own confusion, it is as if we are in darkness. There is nothing we can do about this, unless a first step is taken. A mother can only put food into her child's mouth; the child has to swallow it. It is nature that ensures that the child does this. A child does not need to be taught how to sleep, how to dream or how to think. In the same manner, you do not have to teach a child how to swallow, but you can encourage the child. A similar approach can also help dissolve confusion.

When you are in confusion you become unaware of your own inner resources and potential. Confusion blocks you. You cannot make any decision. Time passes without achievement or fruitful action, because in confusion the wheel of your life rotates without generating currents of joy.

We normally become confused when there are too many issues to be dealt with in a short time, when we have too many choices to be made at a time, when expectations are too high, when there are too many temptations around, and when we fear that we might miss opportunities. This occurs when we do not have the patience to contemplate the issues and our objectives. It is important to understand what confusion is, so that you can take care that it will no longer attack you. A knowledgeable cure is a permanent cure.

The first step to take to overcome that confusion is to seek solitude for a while. For this to happen, you must be attentive and receptive. Be alert and spiritually sensitive, so as to be able to absorb inspirational messages from the universe. Those who are merely academics cannot imbibe such messages, because their lives are determined by words, not by the meaning and the subtleties hidden in them. When you become spiritually sensitive, you absorb the essence of someone's expression from their gestures, accent, tones of voice, actions and vibrations.

Confusion portends that you need to remain in silence and recede into your heart, where intuition is seated. During this time you are only a listener, and some guidance comes, either from higher nature or from deep within you. In this withdrawal of consciousness from the world, stay until the clouds of confusion pass. When confusion evaporates, your vision arises. You become the decision maker. You get strength and courage to make decisions, because you have left confusion behind. Now you have a clear vision. Whenever you think and feel that the vision is dimming you can draw inspiration from people who have realised clarity in themselves, and regain your vision.

It is important to feel your conscious-Self through emotions every minute of your life. When you immerse yourself fully into life, you automatically receive more in return. This applies to every action, since there is no action without a corresponding response, or 're-action'.

Once you are out of confusion, you are able to see clearly. Now, when you want to make a decision, you stop and sit for a while, and you will get a powerful intuitive impulse, 'Go in that direction.'

Our physical body can be scanned. Psychics can make an attempt to read our minds. Astrologers may try predicting our future. However, if we ourselves haven't explored the horizon of our being, we remain ignorant of who we are, and vulnerable to the winds of chance and negative influences. When we allow such influences to affect us, we begin to believe illusions and hallucinations to be a physical reality.

22
Intelligence and Intuition

Intuition is the mother of intelligence. But intelligence, being the naughty child, does not let the mother come in front. Sometimes the mother takes the lead when there is a great need.

Intelligence is generally mischievous by nature. It is the noise of the mind, whereas intuition is the voice of consciousness. Intelligence discriminates, doubts and is restless. It drains your energy and resources and robs you of your time. Unbridled intelligence is destructive in nature. It is like a crazed horse, always racing wherever there are curious temptations. It cannot experience peace and serenity. Common sense, reasoning and logic are the traits of intelligence. It is generally unidirectional, whereas intuition is multidirectional and never confuses us. There are treasures of esoteric wisdom where intelligence cannot enter the most secret zones of our own inner consciousness – whereas intuition, one of the few latent, mystical faculties of our being, can bring forth paraphysical experiences and impeccable answers.

This is the age of intelligence and it has brought with it a great amount of discomfort, misery and instability that has been experienced around the world. Lakes and rivers are contaminated. Forests are being exploited. Deserts are advancing. Many species are becoming extinct. Our lives are becoming increasingly artificial. Technology has entered our bodies. It is a transition.

As we stretch our intelligence, we forget our precious and natural gift of intuition. We are tempted to look outside, rather than into our inner being. Intuition invites us to experience our own hidden potential. When intelligence rests, intuition awakens. Intuition is a self-sustaining and self-guiding force, subject to no master other than itself. It dwells in the heart, while intelligence dwells in the mind.

Intelligence can cause much complication. It is superficial in nature and cannot touch our deep, inner existence. The more we stretch our intelligence, the more materialistic we become. Intelligence alone cannot help us to become spiritual. Spiritual expansion is constructive, and does not give us side effects – those effects are signs of living in the age of intelligence.

Psychic abilities are not the result of intuition. If you want to develop your psychic abilities, you need not necessarily be spiritual. Psychic abilities, such as reading someone's mind or trying to guess the location of a missing object, are advanced mental faculties. In the process of descending from the intellect to intuition, those who give too much importance to psychical abilities are blocked, and unable to descend further. Such abilities alone cannot be guiding forces on our journey, but they can bring entertainment and may give help to some extent. Anyone can develop psychic abilities. All humans and animals are born with them.

All species have certain instinctual abilities, but intuition is spiritual and superior to these. When you expand your intuition you become creative with a firm and constructive foundation. You are receptive to emotional states of different feelings. You experience inner vision and inner voice. Intuition also serves as a bridge between what has already manifested outside, and the various levels of consciousness – including individual consciousness and super-consciousness. If this bridge is broken or damaged, then communication with our higher nature becomes weak. When this happens, the individual consciousness becomes a wandering orphan, without guidance or shelter. With unawakened intuition, our orphaned individual consciousness may become drawn by the gravity of the other side of super-consciousness, or what could be called the anti-super-consciousness, which controls the dark side of creation. When this takes over, those in this situation become negative in their thinking, and disruptive in their approach to life. They become caught up in utter materialism and are unable to experience the subtle gifts of life. Such people may become dictators or tyrants, and cause danger and trauma to humankind.

Usually our society encourages only intelligence, not intuition. From home to parliament and from kindergarten to university, the emphasis is always on intelligence. If this continues, one day our intelligence could become self-destructive. A new-born baby has no recognisable or measurable intelligence. Hence, it has nothing blocking its fresh and eager intuition. It smiles from its cradle. When the baby cries without any apparent reason, this means that intuition has given it a negative suggestion of danger or discomfort. Its smiles indicate intuition has given it favourable or positive suggestions. A baby cannot express otherwise, since it has not yet learned to speak.

Often those who are uneducated have also retained this connection with their intuitive abilities. They naturally and empathetically understand people and easily follow the rhythm of nature. They make their lives simple and highly enjoyable. They live happily with few complaints about others.

When you reach the height of your intuition, you become a realised spiritual being. Intuition can understand what the ears cannot follow and can even hear ultrasonic and infra-sounds. Intuition can smell what the nose cannot smell. The nose can only smell the scent of a flower, the aroma of spices or the odour of objects. It can tell if a smell might be healthy or threatening. Whereas intuition is able to access people deeply through their personalities and smell out their character and feelings. It goes far beyond the visual capabilities of our physical eyes. When we cannot see what is in the distance, intuition can see what lies ahead and provides a guiding light.

Intelligence can only guide our physical movements, whereas intuition can guide our life moments. Intuition can also sense the touch of space, the touch of air, the softness of light and the touch of someone's consciousness. So far, research to further our understanding of the nature and wholeness of intuition, has received little attention. We are only encouraged to study and understand the expansion of intelligence.

Intuition invites one to descend to the heart of our awareness. Anyone can experiment with it. You don't need to go to a laboratory or to refer to handbooks. You don't need a manual to study your own intuition. Any sincere attempt will succeed. You can do this experiment on your own, at any time or place, without any condition, without being religious, and without receiving an initiation. A little attention to our intuition, will help the flower of our life to blossom.

Not only can intuition guide our life, but it can also be applied to assist others, if anyone comes forward needing help. The power of intuition can bring major transformation in a person. Exercising it brings an overall expansion of all that exists within us. It also leads us in the right direction. This direction is beyond the direction of the compass, that which we observe in the outside world. It is a wholesome and harmonious direction, which leads us back towards our origin. The direction it shows each individual is unique. Just as different birds maintain their own routes and altitude, so also each individual has his or her own direction, path and life.

When intelligence exhausts itself, after having used all of its rational resources, you receive guidance to move into the inner realms of the mind, eventually ending up touching the base of intuition, where its voice is finally heard.

It takes some practice and patience to listen to intuition. Intuition really speaks, but it does not use language. For instance, cover your eyes and have someone give you two similarly sized but differently coloured balls, and hold one in each hand. Now let someone ask you the colour of the ball in your right hand. Usually we use our intelligence in responding, thinking of the number of balls we saw in front of us before we were blindfolded, and trying to reason about the probable colour of the one in our right hand. We then make a stab at a colour, and say, 'It is blue,' but when the blindfold is removed we see it is red. From similar experiences we may remember having a sense of, 'I felt that it was red, but I didn't say that.' We used only inference and logic, not intuition. We often regret using logic over intuition: 'Oh, something told me, but I didn't listen.'

We have lost confidence in our intuitive voice because of our centuries-old habit of favouring intelligence. We do not trust our own intuition, even for the sake of experiment. In spite of this distrust of letting our own intuition help guide our lives, we may often trust gambling, lottery and other forms of speculation. One sign of a spiritually evolved being is the trust they have in their own intuition. Intuition is not a faculty of the mind. It can understand the mysteries of life. Undertaking a fast, sitting in solitude, disciplining the body, observing silence, repeating certain special sounds, reading scriptural texts, offering help to the needy – these are all activities that help one to discover the full potential of one's intuition and consciousness.

Sceptics are externally stable but internally disturbed. Their usual approach to the understanding of truth is mainly through doubt and query. We need open-mindedness and sincerity to understand the truth of our existence. We need a receptive and compassionate heart to receive and respond to another's love or call. Intuition can embrace intelligence, but the reverse cannot happen, because intelligence cannot see what really lies beneath its existence.

Our spiritual journey is a process of projecting our awareness deep into our heart, or into the centre of our being. This is not a strenuous or technical effort. It is achieved with ease and grace. You need inspiration to achieve this, but you are taught on your own. It may happen today, tomorrow, next month or in a forthcoming year, but it will happen. Any internal cultivation is never lost, and adds to our true foundation. What we achieve in the outside world is not concrete. It can disappear in an instant, but the experience of your inner-Self is eternal.

There are thousands of questions emanating in everyone's mind every hour. Some are strong. Some are weak. You cannot find answers from reading books alone. When you descend into yourself, you achieve an awakening. Intuition fills your existence, while intelligence curls up and hides. In this state many questions are answered. If this were not true, all people would become followers of intelligence and would continue questioning and doubting everything and everyone. But intuition is a stronger force, and it can be the guiding force in people's lives.

There is an intuitive guiding force in the universe. The earth's orbit is guided. All planets are guided to move on their own paths. Seeds are guided when they are sown in the soil, otherwise they would not germinate. The nutrition extracted from the food in the body is guided. It goes to the respective organs and is absorbed by the correct cells. Intuition can become a major guiding force in one's life.

Now, let us take a deep breath. Assume the main controlling centre is in the heart. *Bring down all energy and attention toward the heart centre.* Tell yourself that you are interested in knowing your own intuition. Say to yourself that you would like to experience your intuition, without suggesting any subject for intuition to address. Just become the spectator and watch. There is so much bright space. Any guidance that arises is not written on a slate or a sheet of paper. It manifests itself in inner space. To continue being receptive, *you must bring your metabolic activities to normal. Do not exert yourself too much physically before entering this state of consciousness. Do not get agitated or excited.* Maintain calmness within. Intuition is innocent, so your approach must be very natural. Intuition always gives justice, whereas intelligence is often prejudiced and partial.

If you are proceeding in the right direction, you see yourself and nothing but bright, beautiful inner space – space full of wisdom, peace and joy. The intuitive zone is pure and sacred, because it is unsoiled by outside influences. Whenever you think you are becoming disturbed, take a deep breath immediately and say to yourself that you are a researcher, a sincere student of the inner science. This process unfolds many great messages, especially designed and created for your own inner growth, which cannot be applied to others.

Receiving inspiration also means charging your own consciousness with the higher cosmic currents. Anything that happens becomes meaningful and uplifting. Your expansion is certain and you feel the fullness of life. Now you realise that 'you' means not just the body or just the mind, but pure consciousness. The rest, you realise, is just an outer cover you have. This realisation becomes firm within as you persist through your inner journey – a silent inner mystical journey.

When you come to the surface of your mind, you become only intelligence. Consider these times as being only a break, or temporary landing, on the physical plane. You go deep again whenever there is the need or invitation from the inner universe. With intuition, learning and achieving something in the outside world becomes easier and natural.

When you contemplate on these inner and outer states of consciousness in solitude, in silence, your pain is relieved. Your questions are answered. Your doubts are dispelled. Darkness turns into light. Intelligence accepts its limitations. Intuition celebrates its victory.

23
The Art of Walking Backwards (Internally)

Walking is not just a physical art with the use of our legs. People with weak legs still walk. It is movement, a gesture of moving into the unknown, into the future; vision is our torchlight; heart beat is the drum of life, a constant reminder of who we are and where we are going.

We make our journey independent, effective and satisfying only when we walk. Our thoughts of movement are translated into action. The will to walk sends profound vibrations through nerve fibres and neurones. The mind and body then co-ordinate to manifest this action. Many people have the will to walk, but the will's vibration cannot pass through their nerves and muscles. The body must be receptive and responsive to the vibration of one's will. Only then can one walk with balance and freedom. People can only walk forward, because our feet are designed this way. It is not safe or easy to walk backwards; nor is it easy to walk sideways. Even the vertebrae of the human body are designed to bend forward. Similarly, human eyes are only set to see forward. You cannot see clearly what is beside you without turning your head. You may roll your eyes sideways, but you cannot have a full or clear vision of objects or people there.

When a baby begins to walk, its innocence begins to recede into the heart and its mind starts to proceed outwards. Though neurologically all human beings walk in a similar manner, there is a noticeable difference in each person's style of walking. People have individual modes and fashions of walking because their natures are different. Their ways of thinking are different. Their tastes and tendencies are different. But walking forward cannot be different. It is the same throughout human existence. Life itself is a walk. Sleep is only a resting point on this journey. Some walk for pleasure; some walk out of curiosity to learn what is happening outside; and others walk for peace, freshness or for health. There are many varied purposes in our walking and, similarly, different conscious species have walked on the earth plane with many different purposes.

Walking is a voyage. There must be a destination, because we all have started our journey from the origin. If our destination and purpose are not understood, then our journey is meaningless. It is like a boat surrounded by a dense fog in the middle of the ocean. It may still sail, but it is not directed.

There is an inborn tendency in every human to look into the future, because of our forward movement. The human body itself is the product of one's past existence. The body therefore reminds us of our past. The mind tends to know about the future, so the mind itself is the future. The inner consciousness, however, is above these two influences. The inner consciousness is pervasive, because it started from an origin somewhere in the past and stretches itself to somewhere in the future. Hence, consciousness is always a present tense. It can become neither the past, nor the future, since these two interpretations are only two-sided. You can walk forward and you can imagine or guess your future, but the future is unseen and untouched. Anything that is not yet experienced is in the future.

No one can see their own back clearly, even with the help of multiple mirrors. The mystery of the future is not in the front as people generally think. The future is in the back. The past is in the front, but it is interpreted the other way around because the human mind is spiritually blind. You can see the past any time, but you cannot see the future. If you want to re-experience your past tense, you cease all your physical activities and the involvement of the mind in the outside world and start walking into the past. This walking is a mystical walking because you do not use your legs. You neither walk on the ground, nor in the air.

When you decide to re-experience all the incidents and events in the past, you have to walk backwards. There is no physical path here to walk on. When you take this mystical walk, backwards from the present to the past, the past becomes the future. Only when you are back to your present tense do you realise you just went into the past, but it still was a journey into the future. To touch the edge of the past, you have to travel. That inner travelling is a journey into the future.

You need time to move. Time for such inner journeys is different from time perceived in the outside world. Though the future of the world, the future of mankind and the future of all species seems philosophically to be one, the future differs from individual to individual. So, also, does the past. What you have perceived in your life in the world is different from what others have perceived.

When you are absorbed deep into your being in order to re-awaken past experiences, you are uninfluenced by the outside world and even by time. At that moment, you have arrested the future. The future is warped because you are going backwards. Internally, it is your future. Externally it is the past. That time, again, is enigmatic. Though you are breathing, your heart is pulsating, the earth is rotating, the physical clock is ticking, your future in the physical world seems still. There is no motion forward because you have gone deep into your past. The experience you have stored about the past is absolutely private. No one can invade it. Unlike computers, which can be accessed with skill and effort, your personal experience belongs exclusively to you. The whole universe itself is walking with giant strides. It is constantly in motion. Our own galaxy is expanding at a very high rate – thousands of miles per second.

In the experience of timelessness of your inner-Self, you connect the two ends of your life, the past and the future, turning them into a beautiful circle. You experience the wholeness of your being and the universe. You become eternally present. Your anxiety, curiosity and physical exertion are all silenced. You walk forward, unaffected by disturbances of the world, such as greed, lust and other negative qualities. Your walk becomes meaningful and effective because you have made your walk a spiritual one. You walk backwards internally at your wish and will, and walk forward in your vision and in the physical world. Your journey completes when the two walks of life meet the timeless.

Part Five
Direct Spirituality

Spirituality is spoken and written about in many different ways, but its experience is direct and often mystical. Gaining that experience is only a matter of time, inspiration and one's choice and effort.

❧ ♥ ☙

24
From Silence to Sound ~ From Sound to Silence

Even a radical materialist feels his or her own inherent spirituality during silence, because silence brings out this forgotten side.

When an action or an event occurs in the universe, it generates ripples of vibrations. Those rippled vibrations are detected by the human auditory nerves, and hence register as sound. The voice of action is called sound. Any action, performed either consciously or unconsciously, creates a ripple of vibrations. This fixed law of the universe cannot be altered or averted.

Whether the sound of the action is harmonious or disharmonious, melodious or noisy, its vibrations always affect the existence of some entity. If you place an animal near a brass gong and strike the gong with a hammer, the vibrations generated from it can disturb the cellular activity in the animal. If the vibrations generated from striking the gong are of high frequencies, the animal may even die.

There is an unrelenting generation of sound vibrations in the universe. It is ceaseless. When sound vibrations are regular in rhythm or harmoniously produced, we accept them and call them music. If sounds are harsh and dissonant and we have difficulty bearing them, we tend to cover our ears. Their deleterious effect on the body and mind cannot be avoided, whether we like it or not. Some sounds, such as ultrasonic and infra-sounds, are impossible for the human ear to hear. This does not mean that there is no production of sound. It means the auditory nerve network in the human ear cannot pick up such waves. This is a great built-in protection of our sense of hearing provided by nature.

If one were to detect or receive all the sound vibrations formed in the universe, one would not be able to sleep, rest or feel peace. Just as an absolute zero temperature is impossible to achieve since there is always some heat energy, so also absolute silence in the universe is impossible to experience. If one went in search of silence, one would never find it. Sound cannot exist without the drum of action, and action cannot take place without producing sound. If there is action, you can always say that there is sound, and vice versa.

Silence is an individual experience. You can ask someone to remain silent, but they may not obey you. In some functions, speakers or programme co-ordinators repeatedly request silence from the audience or participants. By doing so, they only add to the chaos which already exists. You cannot silence others by adding more sounds. You can only hope others will be silenced through your own silent example. You can never achieve this by force. Before we expect others to be silent, we must observe silence ourselves.

The meaning of "observance of silence" should not be restricted to merely being taciturn or remaining speechless. Some may become silent outside but may still be busy in their minds and go through mental chaos though there is silence. But the silence spoken about here has many sides. You can silence yourself by not producing sounds, either mentally or physically. After you decide not to speak to anyone for a period of time, silence will gradually fill your being. You avoid drawing the attention of others as you do not look at them. You minimise your activities. When you walk, you do so slowly and gracefully, without causing any disturbance to your surroundings. Your expenditure of energy is automatically reduced. After a while, you become fully aware of your existence because you are alone. Thoughts that had been incessantly flowing outside are now directed towards the centre. Even a radical materialist would feel his or her own inherent spirituality during silence, because silence brings out this forgotten side.

Your generation of thoughts cannot totally be controlled right from the beginning of your silence, but at least they are not rebounding off other minds, since you are not consciously or directly communicating with anyone. Your silence is a mystic silence. This type of silence is necessary for every individual. When you begin to experience it, sensitive internal organs that were asleep while you were engaged in external activities, are drawn to the surface and their sleeping energies are released. You begin to feel harmony within.

In this day and age, silence suffers heavily from the onslaught of technology. Natural sounds existing in nature are drowned out by artificial sounds. Such artificial sounds affect the body's most sensitive organs. The number of people with heart problems is increasing. This was different a few years ago. Modern man is proud to say he has advanced on a material level; however, health, peace and harmony have declined noticeably. However, the heart can be revived or recharged through silence.

Sound vibrations can damage one's vision. Eyes are as sensitive as the heart, and the cells in them are extremely delicate. Hence, day by day, eye problems are also increasing and the demand for eyeglasses grows. It is difficult to protect your eyes; however, rest and silence can help to energise them. When you are silent, there is no one around you absorbing your energies. Mental energies are also preserved during this type of silence.

Some people are losing their sense of smell because of external sound pollution. Even flowers are unable to give out their scent as naturally and effectively as they were able to as recently as in our own generation. Gradually humans might also lose some of their senses by not keeping them active and alive through natural stimulation. If this continues, it may eventually drive the whole of humanity back to the early stages of evolution.

Silence is at the edge of sounds. Chaos is only the curves and bends of silence, since the beginning and end of chaos is silence. Though sound vibrations prevail throughout the universe, the lover of silence senses spiritual silence through his or her inner silence.

25
Silence – The True Nature of Consciousness

Chaos is only the curves and bends of silence, because there is silence before chaos and the end of chaos is silence.

This seems to be the age of chaos and disorder. The Goddess of Silence, who was resting in the lap of nature before the dawn of science and technology, has been brutally awakened in our modern age. There is diminished hope of experiencing peace, serenity and safety in the world. Loss and damage has already been done to our environment, plants, various animal species and to ourselves. This commotion has caused great physiological damage and psychological impact. There is so much noise in today's life that it is becoming difficult for one to experience serene silence anywhere.

Absolute silence is impossible to feel or sense in the universe. Even in outer space, there is a presence of sound. According to physics there is no space devoid of particles. From a scientific viewpoint, even empty space is filled with anti-particles and virtual particles. These keep colliding, leaving behind some energy.

Wherever there is action there cannot be silence, because there is no action without collision or motion. Action disturbs the harmony of nature. When the harmony or balance is disturbed through action, silence disappears because sound and silence can never co-exist. Just as peace and wealth, love and discipline have difficulty existing together at the same time, so also sound and silence cannot blend together. Wherever there is action, there is noise, because of the involvement of force.

Silence, however, can be experienced deeply within us. An inner receptive space is created through silence, into which insights and truths previously unknown to us may surface. We touch the deeper meaning of our existence. For a sceptic, our existence on earth is due to an accident. For a rational analyst, our existence may be a result of coincidence. For a spiritual person, our existence has a cosmic significance and profound meaning.

We are gifted with the unique ability to experience silence within us. It is a great, cosmic gift. The experience of such in-depth silence is absolutely necessary to our consciousness because silence is the expression of consciousness. Inner silence is elevating and calming. You feel oneness, absolute oneness, when there is a flow of silence. In silence, you feel your spiritual presence because during the experience you become the silence itself. There is no difference between silence and consciousness. You want to stay in that state of inner silence for some time. The experience of inner silence becomes necessary for you to feel settled.

Speaking only when people compel you to speak means silence is very close to you. If you speak only out of your own volition, even though people compel you to speak, there only remains a narrow gap between you and silence, only a hairbreadth of space. When you decide not to speak to anyone for some time, whatever the pressure from others, this means silence has just kissed your face. When you decide not to speak to anyone for a particular period of time, no matter what the situation is, you determine firmly, 'I will not speak to anyone.' You have put a bridle on your tongue to silence it. This means silence has embraced you.

You sit in a solitary place. You place your body in a comfortable posture. You seal your lips. You close your eyes.

You give up food and drink. You do not whisper, murmur, sneeze, wheeze or cough; even your breath becomes barely audible. You have silenced your mind and body. It is a protective silence. You do not worry about the length of time. You sit adamantly. This is a mystic silence. An intimate union occurs between silence and you. The result is the birth of mystical abilities.

Another phase of silence is spiritual silence. But the discipline of spiritual silence is not as concentrated as in mystic silence. In spiritual silence you may not necessarily be in solitude; you may be surrounded by people. Still you are not involved, and you maintain your silence. When someone compels you to talk by asking questions, you simply answer with your gestures and eyes. Here discipline bends, giving more freedom and space for your silent activities.

You look at others but you do not disturb them. If they pass by, you neither ignore them nor do you respond to their looks or words. You do not sit rigidly or firmly in one place. You walk freely. You are engaged in some activity, especially washing or something that indicates cleanliness. The outer cleaning action reflects the inner silent cleansing process of your mind. You sleep or stroll according to your inner suggestion. You do not make any conditions. You stay like this as long as there is no distraction from others. This silence is spiritual silence. Here the effect of silence on our consciousness is relieving and freeing.

You may come out of this silence at any time, or you may extend it for days, weeks or months. You consume food only to maintain your existence, just to subsist. You will not overeat or eat for pleasure, because you are in silence. You do not read or write. You are in silence. That silence prevails within. You are undisturbed and your voice is silent, yet your being speaks. This silence encapsulates all the previously described stages of silence.

This silence is refreshing, energising, pain-relieving and freeing. It has saturated you, like sweetness in honey. Honey itself is not sweet. It is the fructose, a substance within the honey, which makes it sweet. If sweetness itself were honey, then anything that is sweet should be called honey. So your consciousness is like honey. The sweetness of silence is in you – that experience of inner silence is remarkably special. This silence brings freedom, because you are advancing towards Self-realisation and personal illumination.

26
The Meeting of Heart and Mind

Oh my mind, listen to me. I need your co-operation. I need your full co-operation. I want you to be my best friend. I don't want to fight with you any more. This is my purpose. I make a humble appeal to you to listen to my inner voice. Please calm down. Why are you agitated? What are you going to achieve? I am here. I am residing in the heart. Oh my mind, you are always whimsical and unpredictable.

I understand this is not the way to deal with you. Let us negotiate. Let us compromise. Because you are inside of me, our meeting is private. No one can see us. Let us have a common understanding.

Aren't you exhausted? Sometimes you behave like a great scholar, at other times you are worse than a monkey. If I allow you to behave like this, we will both have problems. I want to do so many things. I want to understand so many things. Nothing can be achieved without your sincere co-operation. Love within seems to be frozen because the inner temperature has dropped to zero degrees Celsius and there is no warmth or heat radiation because we are not liasing affectionately.

I have listened to you all these years. Now it is your turn to listen to me. You are like a lover, a wife, a friend – you are everything to me. So listen to me. I may have a thousand plans to implement. I may sit with firm resolution to carry out my work. If you are not totally present in me, how can I fulfil my objectives? I need your support. I cannot complain about you outwardly to others because that just aggravates the situation. You might rebel against me while I am sitting alone in silence. If I share the problems that I have with you with others, you may turn against me and ask me why I criticised you to another. Why didn't I speak to you directly? If a spouse creates a problem at home and the partner criticises him or her in front of their neighbours, it just exacerbates the situation. So I don't want to complain about you to others. Please be pleasant to me.

Many people think that someone has to teach them how to control their minds. This is the equivalent of sending children for lessons on how to behave with their own parents. The tutor would take control of the children and if anything went wrong, he would have to be consulted. This would not be a healthy way for parents to relate with their children.

No one can control the mind or stop its whimsical behaviour. We can only tame it. We can put blinkers over it and make it proceed in a certain direction, as we do with horses. In some meditation methods you may become concerned with the technicalities and mechanics of meditation rather than meditating in your own way – guided by your heart. Some people count their breaths and recite mantras for a specific length of time when they meditate. For them, meditation may become an officially acquired and sanctioned skill or task, instead of a relaxing break or a peaceful experience.

You can achieve peace in many ways. If you sit quietly for a little while, you can find solace. If you change the nature of your work, you may find some peace. When you talk to children, you find more peace and joy, and you may also feel joyous when you watch animals. Most people who have practised meditation for many years are still searching for peace. Achievement of inner bliss, expansion of inner consciousness and realisation of the inner Self could still remain wistful wishes for them.

When you plunge into your inner universe, you learn instinctively through the mysterious guiding forces of nature. No one can live independently of nature, and sustain health or vitality. You may have an ardent wish to remain healthy and graceful, but if the mysterious positive forces of nature were turned against the existing species, the world would become extinct in minutes.

There is no common medicine that cures all diseases in people. If such a medicine were available, everyone would be healthy. What might work for one person, might not work for another because individual constitutions are unique. For example, attitude and aptitude are unique; frequency of energy flow is unique; the structure of your internal, mental network is unique, each person's experience and level of consciousness is unique. Harmonious health can be achieved when we blend spirituality and science in a complementary manner. The day will come when scientists and spiritually evolved people will meet on a heart level, each exchanging with the other their knowledge and experience of different aspects of truth that, together, can transform the earth into a more beautiful planet.

27
Merging the Wave of Life with the Ocean of Consciousness

Life is a wave. Hence it is interesting, exciting and ever graceful. An unrealised human being expects life to be a straight line, unrealistically wanting to be happy every day, without any pain or difficulty. This is not possible to achieve in real life, because it is not the way of cosmic law. One day there is sunshine, the next day clouds cover the sky and it looks grey and gloomy. The following day is sunny again. This kind of cosmic fluctuation is inspiring and educating.

A wave is artistic and creative in its appearance and motion. There is aesthetic attractiveness in a wave, whereas a straight line has no definite message. When the conscious spirit casts off the body, the conscious Self becomes timeless and frameless and the body looks lifeless, cold and still.

There is a rhythmic motion in a wave, just as there is in life. The ocean looks splendid and sublime because of the motion of the waves. Waves in the ocean constantly break, which keeps the ocean clean and beautiful. If there were no waves, the ocean would be dead and uninspiring and as a consequence, all the negative forces in nature would land on the stillness of the ocean and spoil the splendour of the world. But humans generally hope that life will pass without fluctuation, without undulation. They are deluding themselves, because reality involves fluctuation. It establishes one's existence time and time again.

A wave is lively. A straight line is not. There is nothing straight in the universe. It is scientifically impossible to have a completely straight object. There is always some unevenness or roughness on the surface. When you see some objects from a distance, they look smooth and straight, but when you examine them closely, or see them through a microscope, you realise they are not. It is not possible to achieve a straight line. Hence, life is a wave.

The mind wants to make life straight, but this is a mistaken notion. The mind has this desire because it is deeply involved in sensory activities and wants to experience pleasure all the time. If something goes wrong in the body, the mind wants immediate relief. But there can be meaning in certain physical discomfort – it may strengthen and energise the body and eject unwanted elements.

Often a sneeze, cough, fever or pain helps the body become strong. Compare this to road-works, where the traffic has slowed down and is diverted while repairs are carried out. Similarly, the body may need to repair itself from time to time, and one experiences pain for a while. During these times, the sufferer feels his or her complete presence in the body. The mind doesn't tolerate discomfort since it is used to experiencing pleasure through the body.

Sometimes the mind is like a stubborn child. One day if the mother is delayed in attending to her child, the child may become upset, throwing objects and breaking things to express its discontent. The mind makes one cry if one does not attend to it and, as a consequence, a person contorts his or her face even though there may be no good reason. They could experience joy, but do not, because they are slaves to their own mind. Those who have mastered the mind, who have realised that they are pure consciousness, will not be so severely affected by suffering. They know suffering is only a passing cloud. It will disappear. If today is cloudy, tomorrow the sun will certainly shine. It is only temporary.

Many a time we care about ourselves overly; as a result fear and phobia set in insidiously. In the course of overprotecting our physical health we lose the health of our mind and consciousness. Some people are hypochondriacs, lacking inner conviction in their natural curative abilities. Animals relatively do not have as much fear as humans when they are sick. They find their own way to experience relief if humans do not interfere and let them live in their own habitats. They withdraw and sit silently. They retreat into solitude and use their own methods to revive their curative and healing powers. In this respect, animals are closer to nature than humans. Animals have not forgotten their link with nature as we have. Even though humans are supposed to be superior to animals, we would greatly profit by learning from them, our forgotten link with nature.

If they are not disturbed by human beings, animals emit positive vibrations. When they are attacked, tortured and killed, they give out negative vibrations. Modern man is already affected by this in many ways.

Animals know how to protect themselves when they are sick. They exercise their latent, curative energies. They do have consciousness and are able to contemplate themselves and Mother Nature, because they have accepted the reality of life. Human beings have not accepted the reality of life, so they typically worry and wail. You cannot usually rely on them. One day they smile, but the next day they are in a bad mood and will not greet you or speak to you. So you have no security. Your love, your concern and your relationship are distorted and shattered. Only realised beings can maintain the flow of love. They render their service and at the same time, retain their inner joy.

The flow of love exceeds the flow of Niagara Falls. Indeed, the river below Niagara Falls may be frozen in winter, whereas the flow of love can never be frozen. It is always summer for love. Love can even make winter seem like summer. Those who maintain equanimity of mind are reliable people. Those who live only in the confined walls of their minds may desert you when circumstances change, and leave you in trouble.

The art of life is to accept its wave pattern, try to alter wherever one can and to sail gracefully towards the shore of illumination. Few appreciate the skeleton in the body. People think it looks awful, although in reality, it does not. The skeleton is the basis of our physical existence. It is the body's main scaffolding, but the mind has a surface existence and does not want to see such things, or to acknowledge the truth. When we follow the whims of the mind, we drift from the truth and suffer.

The skeleton can be equated to truth. It is reality. The muscles and texture of the skin, well-placed eyes, nose and ears, are all aesthetic arrangements. The mind wants to see the cover through the senses, but in between the aesthetic cover and the skeleton, there exists the conscious Self.

We exist. We experience. And when we joyfully unite ourselves with the rhythms of existence, our life becomes more harmonious, meaningful and secure.

28
Sit, Sit, Sit

Sitting, standing and walking are gestures of your inmost mind. Each gesture bears an abundant meaning to yourself and others; you understand this meaning only when your awareness deepens.

When your space and freedom become contracted, when you are bombarded by outward sounds and thoughts, you become exhausted and want to be alone. You ask people to leave you alone, and you seek privacy. You sit quietly, in a comfortable position. You just sit. No one has forced you to sit. You sit on your own because you wish to sit in that way. All your external physical activities cease. You do not speak; nor do you have any subject to ponder. You sit, doing nothing. At this time you resemble a peaceful lake. You look magnificent like the Himalayas. You are not indulging in any kind of activity, positive or negative. You have no book in your hand to read. You have nobody to converse with. You sit as long as you are not disturbed. You sit as long as you wish to sit. This is the time for looking inside, for introspection.

While you sit, you look serene and special. You look innocent. You are absorbed deeply into your being. You crave nothing. You feel cosy in your heart when you sit like this. You feel unity within yourself. There is less heat energy, because it is an involuntary, silent, spiritual action. At times you keep your eyes closed. At other times you keep them open, and simply blink, not participating in the events that occur outside of yourself. You experience space, freedom, silence and peace within, while you sit. You feel some kind of settling in your heart. You experience a swing between physicality and spirituality.

You are justified in spending time on this activity, because you sit for your own benefit. It brings completion, in the same way as a period does to the end of a sentence. You sit like this before starting a new sentence in your life's history. You look back and ahead. Your heart pulsates with melody. The stream of your blood flows calmly. You become the observer of the movie of your own life. Tranquillity surrounds you, because no serious project occupies you. You simply sit as an act of spontaneity. There is no stiffness in you, only softness and tenderness within. You continue to feel the sobriety of your own sitting posture. There is no one to judge or to comment on your silent act.

You see many things. Your questions are answered in a responsive dialogue with yourself. Those answers are crystal clear. There is no shadow of ambiguity or uncertainty in those answers. Though living in a world of appearances, you are far from the tangible world. You see nothing except your own existence, since all that exists outside yourself is embraced in your heart. You feel absolute oneness. No clock can disturb you, because you are above psychological time. You sit firmly.

You do not know what is happening outside because you are deeply absorbed within. Everything you see belongs to your own life. There is no invasion of alien thoughts. You hear nothing but the sound of your breath and the beat of your heart. You feel the magnitude and omnipresence of your consciousness in each and every molecule of your body. You descend deep into the basic cell units of your physical body. You discover and experience many unknown areas of your horizon.

Before sitting, you were a student, but when you come out afterwards, you look scholarly, because of the spiritual experience it has brought you. In this way, you lead a life of total inner contentment, and you make steady progress. You become a spiritual model for others.

Even though you grow older, you look young, because you remember and retain your inborn quality of innocence. Innocence is youthful. Wisdom is elderly. If you can blend this mature knowledge with the innocence you have at birth, you remain young in your behaviour, attitude and emotions throughout your life.

Part Six
The Curve of Spirituality

Each time you experience consciousness in any form – through love, truth or beauty – you confirm the eternity of your consciousness

᭞ ♥ ᭛

29
The Sweetness of Words

Words are neutral. We add various flavours of moods and emotions. Words uttered casually are dry and uninspiring. Words soaked in emotions carry sweetness and a certain melody, creating an intended image and impression in a person's mind and heart.

Heart and mind are the parents. Feelings and thoughts are their offspring. When a baby starts babbling, the brain becomes the field or abode of thought and mind. Thought and mind interact, producing a growing desire to express. The throat becomes the tunnel from which words gush out. When words are spoken without being edited by the intellect, the speaker will not be understood by others. When words are spoken seriously and forcefully, they take on masculine overtones. When the same words are used sweetly and softly, they acquire feminine qualities.

Such intellect is the epicentre of the mind. Thoughts are like lightning in the sky of the mind, and later they are heard in the form of words. Unlike the lightning and thunder in the sky, sometimes words can remain unexpressed in us. Others will not hear the thunder of these words, but you experience the thoughts. A thought germinates and grows endlessly into a huge tree with countless branches growing in many directions.

When you are in a deep sleep, thoughts remain still and do not reach the conscious mind. When you are in a dream state, thoughts begin to ripple and just touch the conscious mind.

In an awake and very active state, thoughts have strong will behind them and can penetrate throughout and far beyond the conscious mind. When you are experiencing tranquillity and peace, observing nature, thoughts become less intense. When you are absorbed deeply within, they slow down and become steady. Thoughts are personal and private, sometimes within your control but often beyond it. Thoughts are innocent and neutral. On their own, they do not have the capacity to analyse themselves as to whether they are positive or negative. Only the intellect can do this work as a 'bio-conscious' activity.

The brain is like a radio or television, broadcasting sometimes like a satellite station. Thoughts are highly magnetic. When a person consciously and forcefully blocks the tunnel of the throat, thoughts become extremely powerful and, like water, can 'evaporate,' permeating the skull and projecting themselves out into the atmosphere. Some thoughts projected this way are low in frequency, while others are high. Thoughts have a definite form, structure, size and colour. Radio waves are feeble compared to the power of thought waves. Thoughts can travel silently and even faster than the speed of light, since the human brain contains all the complex circuits and necessary resources required for this kind of transmission. You become a communications operator. No walls or fortification can check the motion of thought waves. Today's most advanced scientific inventions are only a grain of sand in the infinite beach of possibilities of conscious brain power.

When you master the art of consciously altering your biochemistry, you become the sculptor of your destiny. It requires willingness and inspiration to understand and unravel the secrets of operating our natural and cosmic 'instrument' called the brain. Whatever is achieved in this manner becomes one's own personal asset, making one stronger and stronger.

When others bring problems to you, you show patience. Your inner calmness remains undisturbed, even by calamitous forces. Your words are sweet and soft like nectar. Each word you utter is imbued with great meaning, conveying your true inner feelings to your audience. *Words are physical; sounds are mystical; meanings are spiritual.* When words are printed or written, they 'fossilise,' becoming cold and rough like snow and ice. They are just ordered stains on paper or computer screens and cannot speak. Being a good reader is not enough to fully grasp the meaning of a word. It takes an expert, a spiritual archaeologist, to animate the fossilised words so that the nectar of meaning can be imbibed.

Generally, people speak without using their intellect to edit what they say. This can cause permanent rifts between family members and even spoil old friendships in an instant like shattered glass. It is difficult to restore friendship.

Once spoken, words can never be taken back. They are recorded in the annals of time. If you are a scholar or a grammarian you choose specific words, arrange them syntactically and express them in a laborious procedure. But if you are a sincere student of metaphysics, if you have identified your spiritual existence, you can express your feelings or thoughts directly through words, using them as scaffolding to convey your abundant meaning. When you speak, you offer much more than mere words. You also use gestures, tone and expression to bring an awareness beyond words to the minds of your listeners. You take every precautionary measure to protect the integrity of your inner meanings.

Your tone is the most important part of your speech. You pronounce effectively, and your tone of voice can refine your words in sweetness when you have awakened your inner love. If that love is not awakened, even if you have a practice of speaking sweetly, you cannot achieve the same sweetness.

Sweetness of tone without love is artificial, like a plastic flower. But with love, your tone acquires an incomparable and rare quality of sweetness such as you have never before tasted in your life. The tongue can only taste physical sweetness, whereas the sweetness of words conveyed through your tone has spiritual nutrition that brings vitality and emotional comfort. Every sentence becomes a maxim. Such sweetness conveys your intended feelings effectively and precisely. Your words are automatically understood by all those who listen to you. Their meaning does not go upward to be reinterpreted by the intellect, but descends directly into their hearts. The words may be forgotten, but the meaning will be retained forever in the depth of their being.

Hearing in this way requires great receptivity. Only when you have an urge to expand your life, broaden your mind, extend the limits of your existence and stretch all facets of your life can this be achieved. It is not like acquiring a degree or a worldly goal. It cannot come by merely asking mechanical questions such as, 'How long will it take to achieve this?' 'How many days should I practise?' 'What time shall I sit and meditate?' It comes through a self-cultivation that has nothing to do with the amount of time spent, but rather with the inner quality of your approach. It has to do with life-satisfying and bliss-experiencing education.

The heart may be clean and one may be honest, but if sweetness is not present in one's expression, words become meaningless and useless. If truth is expressed with this sweetness and with good intentions in a spiritual sense, it becomes universally accepted, without any contradictions or conflict. Even a violent person would immediately mellow and feel grateful when such sweetness is offered. This sweetness brings a wholesome change in life, converting negative minds into positive ones and uniting families. The expression of birds carries this unforgettable sweetness, and this sheds light around you.

For a moment, assume that you are not the intellect, you are not the mind. You are a pure, conscious entity. The heart is the pivot of that consciousness. Love is its centre. Explanation is for others. Experience is for you. In this moment, words are withheld and thought waves are expressed in many ways and in many forms.

Sweetness manifests in you when you express it through singing or dancing. Even if you do not dance because of shyness, your heart still leaps. You cannot stop it. We dance at parties, but rarely do we dance for our own spiritual selves, not to impress anyone, but to celebrate our existence. There is nothing to be worried about. This is an expression of *ananda*.

30
Words, Meaning, Mother (Ma)

Words are like containers in a museum of languages, but meanings are inside ourselves.

Words are physical. Meanings are spiritual. Words hold their meanings as matter holds energy. *Words are like containers in the museum of languages.* When someone wants to convey their meaning, they choose suitable word containers and pour meaning into them. It is not enough for the listener, or recipient, to be aware of the container being sent to them, but they must also look inside it. Only when the meanings hidden in the container are imbibed and absorbed by the receiver, does the communication become full and perfect.

Words are only the carriers of thought-impressions. Meanings come from inside us. We add life and value to words by pouring meanings into the containers of words. For people to convey their full meaning, they must also use many additional qualities – mood, gestures and tone of voice – to accompany and embellish the word containers they send.

Meanings are internal and spiritual. Words are merely physical. In today's world technicians and scientists are busy making more and more advanced fax machines, computers, modems and other technical gadgets, and building satellites and space stations in order to increase the speed and volume of transmitting words and information. But real communication cannot truly happen unless both transmitter and receiver share some degree of spiritual frequency in the exchange.

Words in themselves are not very important, whereas their meanings are extremely so. Words are simply the vehicles for infinite meaning. The present age appears more an age of words than of meanings. When someone offers words filled with meaning and purpose, the recipient, if not hearing on a spiritual level, may carelessly receive these containers, spill their meaning and think they are empty. Such words are only held in the mind. The meaning is lost, and misunderstanding occurs between the two communicants. Although much research is being carried out about the origin of languages, linguistics and the physiological changes that occur when words are uttered, there is still a great deal of miscommunication.

A new-born baby has no vocabulary. It has had no linguistic practice or training. A new-born baby does not even have any idea of its own existence. Yet the first word it utters, no matter what its family's status, creed, colour or nationality, is 'Ma.' When this sound is split, it contains only two letters M and A. There is a gentle mixture of a vowel and a consonant. The consonant M, stretched out by a new-born baby, is physical. The A vowel – very soft, soothing and musical – is spiritual. Without any teaching whatsoever, the baby utters 'Ma' as its first, clear and unambiguous pronunciation. Suddenly, the mother turns her face towards the child. The way a new-born baby addresses and identifies its mother accurately is beyond the comprehension of ordinary intelligence and human conception.

The baby fills this word with a definite meaning. The mother alone receives the full extent of what the baby is saying. The same word, used in different contexts, different circumstances and different tones of voice, conveys different meanings. In discomfort or happiness, the child uses the same 'Ma' word. The baby's mother, no matter what her level of education, recognises and clearly understands each of these meanings. No other person, not even an expert linguist, understands or interprets the meaning of the baby's 'Ma' as well as the mother does. The mother alone has the special internal 'dictionary' giving the meaning of this word, since the communication between mother and child is on a spiritual level. The mother has a thorough understanding of her child, all the way from the physical through to the spiritual levels.

The child doesn't address the father this way, just the mother. Unless the father is spiritually inclined, his communication remains physical, whereas the mother's relationship with the child is spiritual. As the child grows, because of the influence of family members, society and other factors, it gradually forgets this unique 'Ma' word, which carries abundant spiritual meaning, and day by day the child picks up other new words.

After the word 'Ma' is forgotten by the child, the strength of its spiritual communication gradually diminishes. Mother and child continue living together under one roof, but with less and less spiritual communication. They slowly grow apart from each other. Although the child may receive an excellent education from expert teachers and use sophisticated words to convey meaning in addressing its mother, the meaning of 'Ma' is lost. Though the mother can understand her child's sophisticated words, she continues to rely on her intuition and spiritual wisdom. Throughout their relationship, the mother will communicate on a spiritual level, while the child gradually slips from spiritual to physical communication. Even though the child may grow into an adult and become a great scholar, scientist or professor, its main spiritual communication with its mother is gone. The child forgets that its mother, in addition to being its physical origin, was also its original source of inspiration, energy and cosmic grace.

Whether the mother is alive or departed, her conscious positive impression will continue to communicate with her child throughout its existence on earth. But there is no real communication from the child because its 'Ma' has been forgotten. With that one word, 'Ma,' the child would have been able to communicate everything it desired. It would have been used thousands of times to express so many different shades of meaning, and the mother would have understood each one. Without communication with the mother, there can be no blessing, no grace, no inspiration and no protection.

In your heart, when you remember with utmost sincerity that word 'Ma,' you will pronounce it in the same internal, silent and mystical way, and once again reconnect your communication with your mother and with the Mother of mothers. Spiritual communication is re-established. When this communication is in place and is once again perfect, then other communication in the material world can also be meaningful and significant.

31
Desire – Dream of the Awakened Mind

Desire is the seed of the dream. Seeds of desires grow into a huge tree; only sometimes you reap the fruits of dreams in wakeful states of consciousness.

Desires are free-flowing but actions are rigid. Desires are more sensitive than the wind. Many unfulfilled desires are fulfilled in dreams. The submerged mind creates its own world and uses the surface mind as a screen for its projections. In this process the surface mind divides itself into characters, images, objects and so on. In this show, you become the audience.

Desire, when inflamed and negatively distorted, becomes greed. Desires can emerge and ripple out from you at any time. Desires use your mind as the pen, and space as the paper. As they grow further, gathering heaviness, they descend into your deeper consciousness, and wait for the time and opportunity to urge you to do things in the real world. If desires are unattained, or unattainable, in the physical world, they express themselves in dreams and then vanish.

Desire is a powerful force. More powerful than the mind. More powerful than the body. And more powerful than the intellect – where logic and reasoning are thrashed out. A single stimulus can create numerous desires. Some desires come as faint whiffs, which just linger in our mind briefly and then disappear, while other desires persist for some time before dissolving. Few desires settle deeply in the mind.

Desires always set us in motion and rarely bring us bliss and peace. With them we become wanderers. So, practising withdrawal of our senses from the outside world can reduce the quantum of stimulation. This may help us to maintain clarity of mind and an ability to stay above, or to withstand desires, and to create a protective invisible shield around us. In this way, we can guard ourselves from outside attack, and realise how we had previously been manipulated by the fantasy of desires. Before spiritual realisation, we were restlessly tossed by the tides of greed and desires. After realisation, we focus all our inner resources on becoming deserving. With the increase in deservedness, many gifts come into our lives, but we remain unaffected.

Let the boat of life sail smoothly, and the tides of illusion drift away from us. May our vision and action be harmonised.

32
Your Mystic Space

The universe outside yourself is a scientific reality and a rational understanding. The universe is within you is a mystical reality. 'I am the universe' is a spiritual experience.

Every human being has his or her own inner space. This space is different from the space spoken of in physics. Individuals carry their own individual space with them wherever they go. It is exclusively their space. This space is elliptical in shape and is larger than a person's body. It can spread itself, penetrating any object. Nothing can contract a person's space. Even if the person is encased in an iron cell, their space will still penetrate the iron and maintain its true form.

This elliptical and individual space, unknown to physicists, and unique to each individual, is filled with fine, vibratory particles. These highly refined particles vibrate in different frequencies around the person. Although the vibration of these fine particles varies from time to time, the frequency of vibration remains more or less the same throughout one's existence. These extremely subtle and fine, live particles carry information of one's past, present and future.

This elliptical outline of space has various shades of colours. When a person is very agitated, or angry, it turns red. When a person has a balanced energy level and a clear understanding, it is green. When a person is calm, poetic and creative, the colour changes to blue mixed with black, with the blue dominating. When a person has developed mystical, or occult powers, then their unique elliptical outline of space shows as yellow or gold all over. These shades of colours cannot be seen with human eyes, because those eyes are designed only to see physical light that stimulates the retina. Even in physical light there are many shades that are invisible to the human eye; for instance, ultraviolet and infra-red light cannot be seen by unaided human eyes. If the human eye cannot detect certain sensitive, physical light radiation, then how can that same eye perceive mystical light? It is a light that differs from any known physical light.

Human existence is nothing but a spark of light. This light has awareness. It is a conscious light. This light has splintered from the giant, brilliant cosmic light that is more powerful and brighter than the flash of lightning you see in the sky. There are various forms of conscious existence. For example, scientists have found traces of living beings on Mars. Even though those beings did not necessarily have the same form of body we possess, the core of all living beings is light.

The body is only something of a capsule for that light, like an electric bulb. An electric light bulb is so flimsy and fragile that you can easily break it, but the spread of its light is many times larger than its own physical outline. Similarly the human body is fragile and brittle. Even particles of dust or minor discomforts are enough to disturb it, yet the role and responsibility of humans on earth is immense.

Though our physical body is fragile and vulnerable, we carry mountains of desires and ambitions and become uncontrollably mischievous, indulging ourselves in destroying beauty, peace and even the lives of other beings.

The body is only a location, like a co-ordinated point in space. A person can move his or her body in whichever direction he or she wishes. But, instead of physically moving, a person could also imagine travelling to other places. This kind of journey takes place faster than the speed of light.

Surgeons see the body as a machine, and they scan, dissect and study it only from a physical point of view. This cannot reveal the whole truth. Hence, science is unable to diagnose precisely, or to find exact cures for the varying ailments of the body. On the other hand, spiritually advanced beings, those who have expanded their consciousness, are doctors of the inner body. They can scan, bring inspiration and offer some mystic hints, increasing one's strength and stamina, even influencing biochemical activities or physiological functions to some degree.

Human existence is not just physical. A human being is a dot in the centre, surrounded by an elliptical space. This space is a natural protection given to us by higher nature. If we had no such space to guard us, we would not live as long as we do on the earth plane, facing the possibility of many accidents and injuries.

It may be easy to be born, but it is difficult to die. Death is not as easy as people think because that elliptical space has gathered much experience on the earth plane, fulfilled many ambitions, and generated many wishes and desires. It has developed strong attachments. Furthermore, there are people who hold on to others internally, not wanting to let them go. A person's existence becomes a collective one, rather than remaining just an individual one, as family members, friends and relatives extend their profound desires, making them retain their physical presence – their capsule of light. It is also for this reason that a person medically diagnosed as having a defective body, may surprisingly live for an extended period of time, although their continued existence can seem to be a miracle and a mystery.

This mystic space becomes protective. It expands only when we enhance our conscious power through spiritual practices. You may call it *sadhana*, or *tapasya*, or *dhyana*. In whatever form, the colours that manifest around a person in that space look bright and clear.

You first see lightning in the sky, and only after a while hear the sound of thunder, because sound travels slower than light. Similarly, an effect occurs first in one's field of space, and then echoes in the body. It is possible to foresee an event or incident that might happen, and before one suffers emotionally, physically or socially, take precautions to prevent it or prepare oneself to face it. Whatever we see in the body is old news. First it occurs in that mystic space. Then it manifests in the physical space, the body. Those who are spiritually advanced can understand and see a person's whole personality through that space. They may even catch glimpses of future events.

People who go away from spirituality lose protection, because this space around them becomes weak and deteriorated. Then they become vulnerable to invasion from the outside world. There is an opposite force to life. Negative forces in nature may be called black forces, or even anti-existent forces. Such forces create illusion and disturb one's faith, trust and confidence. With them, you might lose contact with your real Self. The mystic space becomes blurred. As a consequence, peace and bliss evaporate.

When you sit quietly on your own with closed eyes, even for a brief period, you note many positive changes in yourself. Some people may have maintained a good physical appearance by going to a gym regularly and toning their muscles, yet they may look weak and fearful. They may not have realised or strengthened their mystic space and may believe only in their physical strength. Some people are not physically strong, yet they protect themselves, live long and experience many things in their lives, because of the strength in their mystic space.

33
Time from the Timeless

When you are engaged in celebration, you become ageless, youthful and timeless; you become time-bound when you do not recognise something unique in you.

The moment the conscious spirit lands in a single primordial, biological cell, the count of time begins. With the count of time, the manifestation of that conscious spirit through the physical form intensifies, resulting in birth. As the wheel of life rolls on into infancy and adolescence, a person is able to discern and discriminate between the three sheaths of time: past, present and future. Consciousness perceives the different sheaths of time through the mind, and then flows out in words, thoughts and actions.

The past becomes concrete, because there is a solid experience of events that have occurred in one's life. The senses have been propelled through time. Since the body has grown with the count of time – biologically, psychologically and philosophically – the past becomes an ingrained and unalterable experience.

The present is abstract. Intellectually it is interpreted as a reality but consciously, or spiritually speaking, the present has no resting place, since the whole cosmos is in motion. Every particle is constantly vibrating. All species are in a process of growth and decay. Thus, present time is actually a concept – a personal perception and a subjective experience, not open to interpretation and scrutiny. It is a vantage point from which we view time. There is actually no rest at all. The body is in full action, and there is unrelenting movement in life. Even when one is in a deep sleep, the body is still alert, and even the submerged mind is on guard. The inner, conscious Self is aware of everything that happens in and around one's physical being. That never ceases. Everything is in complete action. Hunger, thirst, death, time and space are undeniable co-ordinates in the eternal.

Humanity has no freedom to alter these inflexible cosmic principles. We have no choice since our very existence is the essence of all the cosmic laws. The past is behind one's existence. The future lies ahead, yet to be experienced but mystically it is the opposite. The motion, or the rolling of the wheel of life, cannot be halted, not even for a minute period of time. The future is unseen. It can be inferred or guessed vaguely, but not accurately, since it is not dependent on a single person's nature, thoughts and decision. The future has already unfolded throughout the cosmos. The earth has to complete its orbit. Life has to be experienced. The sun has to generate energy. All species have to complete the cycle of the everyday experience of wakefulness, dreaminess and sleepiness. Even going to sleep is an action. The future reflects an interconnectedness between all individuals, so that the decision and action of one single person can affect another person, several people, or even the whole world. Nobody literally travels into the future, the future actually comes closer and closer, and then moves into us – and, yet, there will still be things untouched, not yet experienced and continuing to unfold.

The past is old. The future is young. The future is mysterious because it creates a veil before our eyes. It makes life exciting and interesting, with the questions, 'What will happen? How will it happen? When will it happen?' With the understanding and experience of the fine lines of triangle of time, internally, in our inner minds and hearts and in our vision, we remain ever youthful as the present, because we realise the timelessness of consciousness. The past, present and future are only the affectations of the mind and body. The consciousness that one observes in a new-born baby is the same as that in an old man about to exhale for the last time. Consciousness embraces the present, because it is all-pervasive. When the mind gives up, consciousness dawns on what cannot be intellectualised or conceptualised. Consciousness can invite and sustain infinite experiences.

Until you descend from your mind and body to your own field of consciousness, you only think about what has been experienced mentally and physically. There are many things of which the mind cannot imagine even a fraction, because such infinite cosmic experiences are beyond rationality, reasoning and logic. We cannot calculate with precision the number of cells existing in the human body, or the length and strength of the human nervous system. There are many limitations in understanding our surroundings and ourselves. Just a thin fog can restrict our field of vision. If we are busy talking while eating, the tongue's taste buds cannot detect the diverse flavours of food. Different facets of physical and mental experiences occur beyond the range of the senses, and are experienced only when one plunges into the depths of one's consciousness. When you close your eyes, you can feel the opening of the inner mind more intensely.

Every individual has his or her own way of gaining such experiences. Inspiration can help one to reflect one's own consciousness. Inspiration is the power that awakens the energies that sleep beneath the known mind in all of us. Our consciousness waves in the breeze of inspiration.

Rock artists and philosophers cannot flow from their heart unless they are inspired by romance or something higher. The source of inspiration can be anyone or anything. This source can also be a gesture for us from nature, to open our minds, to unfold the petals of creativity, intuitive wisdom and insights of all that we want to know and experience.

34
Miracles

A miracle is just a glimpse of super-conscious laws. It can be empowered in one's being only when there is receptivity or conductivity. The true miracle is the transformation from negativity to positivity, from scepticism to spirituality, from cynicism to love-experience and from reasoning to realisation.

Miracles are indescribable phenomena. They are beyond rational thinking and scientific understanding because their very nature is mystical. Logic and reasoning are overpowered by miracles, which cannot be interpreted by the human intellect.

Miracles pass through the mind in a flash, leaving an everlasting and positive impression on consciousness. The intellect is like a lawyer. It can argue but not give judgement, while intuition can make silent judgement. The heart is the home of intuition.

Miracles re-establish trust in one's conscious power. Miraculous experiences are the foundation for many religions in the world. You cannot share your miraculous experiences with anyone, because miracles that happen in your life are specifically designed and suited to your personal needs and level of conscious evolution. Others will not be able to understand and appreciate what you have experienced.

The mind is like a balcony. You come out and sit on your balcony to watch what is happening in the world. It is like a communication centre or junction between minds. It is a meeting place to exchange ideas and thoughts. But you only stay on your balcony temporarily. When you are tired of being on the balcony, you go into your personal sanctuary, which is the heart. This is a very private room. You can do whatever you want in your heart, without anybody seeing or knowing. There is no possible danger from the outside world, because you can shut the doors of your balcony and enter your personal chamber. Intuition dwells here, in the heart. Apart from giving messages and guidance from within, intuition also has the ability to receive wisdom through miracles.

Personal experiences of miracles cannot be described verbally. They act as a wake-up call. You become alert. These personal experiences come after you have applied and exhausted all your inner resources to achieve your wishes, and you give a profound inner call, because you have climbed the stairways of all possible physical effort and endeavour and reached the final stage. You are now prepared to receive higher gifts. Your call is sincere, because you have spent everything you have within you to achieve the intended goals. Now you are prepared, you have become a recipient for great miracles. The sound of your call echoes in your heart and in the heart of super-consciousness.

When someone's heart fails, an electric shock or a heavy thump on the chest is administered to awaken the sleeping organ. Similarly, when inner consciousness becomes shrivelled, the touch of a miracle can re-establish its power. The first miracle is that you entered the earth plane. One single mistake would have been enough in the complex embryonic process to stop you from entering the world. That it did not happen is the first miracle. You might have been just a weed or a pebble, but that did not happen either. You are here in human form to experience life. Is this life not worthy of celebration?

In spite of this, humanity still splutters with scepticism because we stay on the balcony of the mind. There were many times in life when you were surrounded with the fog of confusion and calamity, and you could not remove yourself from a situation. Something guided you to hack your way through all the tough twists and turns. The fact that you managed to ride out those rough times is also a miracle. There are many more miracles yet to come when there is need or when you are prepared.

Another noticeable miracle is that all planets are suspended beautifully and systematically in space, like colourful balls. This is the miracle of centrifugal force. How exquisitely stars are distributed in space to bring inspiration and cheer! People rarely have time to appreciate and adore these miracles, but we make time to invite problems and make things more complicated. We also have time to worry about many things. The human brain is just an activated lump of flesh, but it is the medium and gateway to understand and experience oneself and the universe. Is this not a miraculous gift?

No one is pushing the earth, but still it orbits the sun. No one is sprinkling water, but the rain still comes. No one fans the world, but the wind blows. When we are hungry, we know how to chew and swallow our food, and the nutrition is distributed and assimilated throughout the body even though we are not consciously aware of how this takes place. Why do we not wonder at these phenomena? We take them for granted since they occur closely and commonly, but they are perennial miracles.

35
The Cosmic Tree

Everything in the universe, whether it be terrestrial or celestial, is governed by fixed laws, such as gravity. The energy in the nucleus of an atom, the number of particles in a vacuum, birth and death are all fixed laws of nature. These laws are stubborn. They do not change. And yet, these stubborn, cosmic laws give birth to flexible beings. It is like the hard trunk of a banyan tree; its roots are firmly fixed deep in the ground, but its branches spread in many directions. Such hard roots and trunk can give birth to delicate leaves that quiver when the wind blows.

The trees that we see in the physical world are not the same as the tree of the cosmos. The cosmic tree is inverted, with its roots at the top and branches at the bottom. This is the reality, but we perceive it differently since we are earthbound and confined to local gravity.

All conscious beings in the cosmos are the tree's fruit; all stars are its leaves; all directions are its branches. It is a vast cosmic tree. It is a paradox that the inflexible laws of the cosmos give birth to flexible beings. If conscious entities are not flexible they cannot live. They cannot perform actions. The ego that exists in all conscious entities is stubborn because it is representative of its root in higher space. It is the anchor of ego that holds all conscious beings in the cosmic tree.

The ego is the only communicative thread between an individual conscious entity and the super-conscious. You are the ego, where 'you' means the wholeness of your being. It could be the mind; it could be the body; it could be your nature; it could be anything existing in you. The ego is fixed and generally manifests itself when you are provoked or enraged, or when you are truly loved by someone. You cannot distil your ego. As DNA decides and guides the shape, size and features of the body, so also the ego, being the mystical DNA, guides the outline and attitude of one's mind.

The body is not completely flexible because its infrastructure is firm. The skeleton is your body's scaffolding. There is no need to be afraid of one's skeleton because it is internal. The body does not have complete flexibility because it is the trunk of the ego tree. It is a fact of physical existence.

Not all people show interest in knowing the physical truth of their own being. You will achieve enlightenment only when you know the truth or make a courageous attempt to discover the truth. Fallacy can give temporary relief or momentary satisfaction. Fallacy is tempting, but truth is comforting.

Then there is mind. The mind has to be flexible in order for you to comprehend anything. Without flexibility you cannot react, imagine, remember or feel anything. The heart is even more flexible. When people touch your heart, you will flow towards them, like a river. You will just melt and float in their direction and, although you have your own existence, love will enable you to become one with them.

The heart is free and flexible. The heart is sensitive to cosmic signals, cosmic radiation and the subtleties of emotions and feelings. Unlike the heart, the mind tends to perceive negativity. The mind takes a long time to welcome truth or true emotions. The heart is always ready to welcome truth and to invite love experiences. Our physical body is limited in sharing physical time and physical presence, whereas our spiritual heart is vast and spacious and can accommodate all that is good and beautiful. That is the power of the spiritual heart, because it is deeper in its nature. Furthermore, it leads us to the conscious understanding and experience of life, nature and the universe.

Consciousness can combine inflexible and flexible laws. Consciousness can experience or embrace both flexibility and inflexibility. If you want to draw a circle, you have to start somewhere. You cannot simply draw a circle without starting at a particular point. You will come to know exactly where it is located only after drawing the circle. The beginning point is fixed but the rest is flexible and the line of the circle meets at the same point of beginning. That is the power of consciousness. It can take both flexibility and inflexibility, in the sense that these two different natures in the cosmos are embraced by the individual consciousness. No law can govern your consciousness.

Consciousness is always superior to intellect. Each time you experience your consciousness in any form – through love, truth or beauty – you confirm the eternity of your consciousness. Spirituality is closely associated with consciousness. The human intellect attempts to understand the physical nature of the cosmos. But the metaphysical nature and quality of the cosmos can be realised and experienced only in the field of one's consciousness, through the heart.

This is not a physical action but a silent, internal, mystical action, which results in expansion of consciousness. This process is spiritual because it is achieved silently, within, through your own sincere endeavour. Your expansion in a material sense is not independent. You need people to praise you. You need people to reward you. You want people to understand your ideas and believe in your abilities, but this is not always possible in the world. Hence, there is often misunderstanding, miscommunication and conflict in human society. Sometimes harmony is difficult to achieve even in a single family – how can one expect to find it on a larger scale?

Spirituality is independent. You do not need external resources in order to realise the potential and power of your consciousness. You are beyond time, beyond seasons and beyond anything you see in the external world. If you are rigidly religious you need a specific time to offer your prayers, a fixed time to undertake a fast, a prescribed time and location for the performance of rituals or the reading of sacred texts. Whereas in internal spiritual experience, study and experimentation are totally independent and you are self-resourceful.

Once that spiritual awakening occurs, it will never cease. The mind may become confused, but the heart, which only records experiences, is always clear. The heart can preserve the most sensitive impressions of super-sensual experiences but this is not yet understood by modern researchers, who spend most of their time probing into the physical components and functionality of the body. *Spirituality is a self-expanding process towards the realisation of the Self.*

Experiencing oneness means to bring the body, the mind, the senses, the consciousness and the heart to unity. The moment you experience oneness, even for a brief moment, your heart is filled with energy. This oneness is powerful. We can build houses and live safely inside because of the unity in atoms. If they didn't cling together properly, we wouldn't have any physical protection or shelter in the world. Oneness is an experience of inner unity.

Anything you experience is spiritual. Anything you explain is physical. In the course of gaining experience about the world our senses respond to stimuli from outside. They are received as signals by the brain and translated into information. This information filters through to the subconscious mind, but the subtler impressions are trapped in the heart region. The undigested information is diffused through a person's energy field.

As you progress in your personal spiritual training, fear fades away. Expansion of consciousness is not like the expansion of a company. You gradually become aware of your conscious evolution. If you don't show hatred towards others, if you are not greedy, if you are receptive to truth and if you can sense innocence and goodness in others, you have prepared yourself. You are on the verge of the mind and on the threshold of the heart. Any time you wish, you will slide into the heart for beautiful conscious experiences of various forms of your own existence.

36
The Triangle of Life

Birth and death are like the wave and trough of an eternally moving wave of consciousness in the infinite ocean of cosmic consciousness.

Disease, decrepitude and death can be represented as the three sides of the triangle of life. The three lines that form the triangle repel each other and do not quite join, resulting in six ends. These ends represent the five basic elements in nature: fire, earth, water, air and ether, or sky. The sixth end represents genetic shelter, which signifies the first cell of our physical existence. Conscious life force is like a circle at the centre of this triangle.

Three gates are formed in this representation. These gates are like sentinels through which conscious life force, which can come from any direction in the universe, can be invited. This conscious life force is a pulse of invisible light, which enters the inner space of this unjoined triangle.

Conscious life force is itself an entity, albeit invisible, that exists somewhere in the universe and is unaffected by the laws of the physical world. As that conscious life force enters into the periphery of the inner, triangular space, the three gates are automatically and firmly welded together by cosmic forces. Hence, being born is the involvement of the conscious life force in matter, and leaving the body may appear difficult because conscious life force has become enmeshed in matter and experience.

You might lend your property to someone, but later, you may find it difficult to retrieve it, because of sentimental attachment. Similarly, it is not easy to leave the body.

The cosmic life force descends into the triangle that has the circle within it. You may call the circle a zygote, or primordial cell. It has all the information necessary to form a physical conscious species, be it animal or human. The triangle is minute at this stage. Gradually, it multiplies itself into an infinite number of triangles.

Human beings exist between the microcosm and macrocosm. Humans cannot exist on a microcosmic level, because cells are dying in the body every second. If we were to exist microcosmically, we might exist only momentarily, because the life span of cells is short. Nor could we exist macrocosmically, since this would require a gigantic body and a change in the concept of time and space. There would be morphological changes, and the thinking process would differ significantly. We would have to devour enormous amounts of food. The volume of space required would be very large, so the population would have to be less and, proportionate to that, everything would have to change. The outer environment would have to be accommodated, resulting in ecological change. Maybe the Earth and our environment are not destined for that kind of existence. So, humanity exists in between these two levels of the universe. This is the reason we can understand beings on a lower level. At the same time, we can raise our consciousness and conceive of the probability of higher beings.

A person's entire span of life is like a day. Birth is the dawn of life, and childhood is its morning. This explains why most children look lively and cheerful. They are eager to get acquainted with their surroundings. There is elation and excitement because it is the morning of life. Children usually want to touch everything that comes their way. They want to gather new information by turning on the television or reading newspapers, looking for an opening message to start the day. Youth is the meridian of life and therefore is very hot. There is much energy, but there is less wisdom and experience. Wisdom and experience can be received from elders, but young people do not like to do that, because of the generation gap. The time between youth and old age is the afternoon of life. One's nature and behaviour change in the afternoon of life. At an advanced age, one experiences life's evening. Hence, in their mature years, most people look peaceful and composed.

Only half of death is visible. The other half is invisible, or beyond the mind. Death is a relief from the 'day of life,' and conscious life force again moves back into the earth plane, or to other planes of existence, or to wherever there is willingness to move on to a new project and new galactic attire, to start life once more.

Similarly, in life, from one birthday to another is just one hour. You take a break on your birthday because it is a transition time. Though time cannot be stopped, you can withdraw from your routine activities. When you sit in a pensive mood, contemplating what has been and what is to come, many friends, family members and well-wishers come to you just to let you know you are not alone on your journey. They are all there to share your experiences, wisdom, love and everything that is possible to share. People come on your birthday just to give. If you can absorb their love and good wishes, you realise what a king or queen you are. Wherever you walk is your kingdom. Wherever you sit is your throne. Your head is your crown. Your hands are your gauntlets. You use them to protect yourself and your beloved ones. Your feet are your horse. After this realisation, you also recognise others as the same, and you adore them. If you are a woman, the heart becomes your king. If you are a man, the heart becomes your queen.

37
Dhyana – Experiencing and Understanding the Invisible Side of Life and the Universe

The mind emerged from the convergence of the body and consciousness. It came with the intention of assisting you, but broke its promise because of the negative influence of the world.

D＊*hyana* is an exercise – a silent, mystical exercise of your consciousness.

The underlying purpose of *Dhyana*, or fine meditation, is to rise above all rules, conditions and disciplines of the physical, to experience the freedom of the Self.

Anything you make monotonous in your life lacks vigour and sweetness. Make your life special! The experience of *Dhyana* is always new and unique. Each time you descend into *Dhyana*, you feel the vibration of your conscious life force and gain a new experience. Sit only when you feel an inner urge. The true experience of *Dhyana* is always spontaneous and inspirational. Spiritual height cannot be achieved through physical discipline alone. *Dhyana* is a deep absorption in nature – both inner and outer; it is the experience of consciousness through one's heart.

Why do you like life? It is because every day brings newness and surprise. These are the pulses of our life. Just imagine if each day were the same, with the same weather, and conversation, and the same circumstance. Would life be interesting? We need progressive change. We need a break from the monotony of life. We all want to remain special and we deserve this. The universe has bestowed upon us everything we require to feel the special essence, nature and qualities of life. Let us make life a festival! A celebration!

We are growing, ageing, changing and evolving. Life began from a single cell that multiplied myriad times and emerged into this full form of existence. When this was complete, human consciousness evolved.

The human physical brain is three-dimensional, but the mind is multi-dimensional; it uses the brain, the nervous system, energy and all the resources within us as its medium. We have enough information to look after our physical well-being; now we also need inner growth and conscious expansion.

The mind is intangible and impalpable, because it is beyond our own perception. If the mind fails to function due to illness or injury to the brain, external voluntary activities cease. Such is the case during a coma, where the mind has receded into the deeper layers of our nervous system. We cannot experience anything in this state. We cannot respond to the outside world, because the mind is the gate to the conscious world. We use many techniques in order to experience the mind and its roots, but we are rarely successful. In attempting this, we go against natural laws, and so are rarely rewarded.

The mind is very sensitive. Its movement is more subtle than that of mercury. As the mind is so sensitive, delicate methods must be used in order to master it. The mind is like the wind. The wind cannot stay in stillness for long. The wind has to blow, and the mind has to flow. You can tame your mind, but you cannot control it. You cannot stop your mind, but you can steer it. There is no analogy for such sensitivity.

It is undeniably necessary for our mind to be like this for our physical existence. How can you still your mind, when the seat of the mind, the brain itself, is so intricate and complex in its network, chemistry and function. Control of mind and severe concentration are the emphasis of most meditation techniques. In *Dhyana*, the mind becomes your obedient servant. Your senses become observers. Your consciousness sways, and abundant energy is released.

The mind is both useful and dangerous. Like a knife or any sharp instrument, it must be used with care. If we mishandle a knife, we may suffer injury. It could even be life-threatening. The mind is not only your friend, but at times it may also turn against you like an enraged elephant. You cannot ask anyone to control your mind; nor can you control it yourself. If you want to unfold its mysteries, you have to tune in to the wave pattern of your mind and become one with the flow of your thoughts. Do not force it to listen to you; it can be tamed smoothly and gently. If your mind is agitated, simply take a rest, remain silent and if you feel the need, go into solitude for a while. Consequently, the mind will settle itself and you will see a noticeable difference.

Your mind is usually the first target of any disease. Then the disease filters through the various strata of the mind to the layers of the body. If poison enters your body and the mind is not aware of it, its harmful effect is often delayed. Similarly, if someone convinces you that you have an ailment, even if it is not true, you may generate a psychosomatic pain for some time. This can be more severe than real pain.

When we master our minds, we become sensitive to our intuition. Generally, we do not listen to the inner wisdom of our body, which speaks to us when we are ill and weak. If we do not listen, how can we then expect good health, harmony and peace? When we do not listen to these instinctive and ordinary physiological and psychological signals, how can we understand, receive and interpret the finer intuitive signals transmitted from deep within?

Rather than listening to our bodies and other signals from within, we often tend to impose our opinions on others. In doing so, we hinder our own progress and that of others. Through *Dhyana* we can experience spiritual freedom, not by entangling ourselves in mind techniques, but by becoming deeply absorbed in the innermost expanses of our heart and consciousness. This brings about peace, realisation, joy and wisdom.

If you lay down some conditions or rules for *Dhyana*, you will return to the physical and will not be able to experience the spiritual. Therefore, specific techniques have not been outlined to enter the state of *Dhyana*, because everyone has to find their own ways of expanding consciousness. However, many hints and tips twinkle throughout this book as an inspiration – to improve the reader's understanding and experience of spiritual awareness. Please identify or map out the route of your own life. Everyone's path is unique. Each person's mode of journey, dimension of consciousness, perception, concept and process of time, and frequency of bodily vibrations are different.

During the process of *Dhyana*, keep your eyes closed. Take off any glasses and wristwatch, and empty your pockets of anything that might cause you discomfort or distraction. Feel free and relaxed. Do not make your posture of *Dhyana* stern and stiff. You may sit comfortably, or you may lie on the floor. There is no fixed or recommended posture for one to enter *Dhyana*. In the beginning, you may fall asleep. This does not matter; it means the body needs sleep and rest in order to feel fresh. After a time, this will not happen.

Keep your eyes closed so as to be ready to travel into the inner world. Be as comfortable as you can. Let there be some quiet place for you to relax and express your feelings. It is unnatural for you to inhibit your heart. This leads to confusion and further suffering, which may build up pressure. Draw your attention away from the mind towards the heart, the centre of your existence. This is not the physical heart, but the centre where you experience deep feelings and emotions. In *Dhyana*, the unexpressed inner feelings can be expressed and released. This allows you to regain your spiritual identity.

Now, take several deep inhalations. When you exhale, empty out all that causes heaviness in you. Some people are moved to tears. Others may smile. Some gracefully move their hands, while others feel a floating sensation. There are many ways to express yourself in *Dhyana*. Do not make any special effort to control yourself. Simply be yourself.

Follow whatever inspiration you receive without limiting yourself. Keep your heart open. Feel the rhythm of your heart, the flow of naturalness and love. Let everything flow, otherwise you could miss the opportunity of experiencing something special and intuitive.

In *Dhyana* there is no specific subject or object for you to concentrate upon. You flow freely, and you may experience feelings of high spirit and elation. In this process, you will come to know the depth of your own consciousness. We are all natural, conscious beings. We are all pure consciousness. In this state, you unite everything that comes your way and fuse all that is within you into a single entity. After this experience, you see the same unity in the outside world. You do not see much negativity, because you have experienced oneness.

After your daily routine of duty in the world, you return to your home, close the door and relax. In the same way, when you are exhausted with the physical world, after spending much energy and time, close the door of your senses and shut the window of your mind to reach your inner being with focus and conviction. Here you are secure and can relax comfortably.

When we realise this as our true, inner home, we reforge and reconnect our link with it. When this communication is cut off, we feel alone, confused and insecure. We usually think we preserve everything only in our brain or mind, but truly, whatever we keep in our heart is special and can dwell there throughout our life. Then, whenever we are exhausted and feel it is necessary, we can evoke this sweet memory, recreating the same world within and regaining everything we felt was lost.

Cosmic forces are ready to assist anyone in their progress. Only those who experience such assistance know the efficacy and fruitfulness of this inquiry and exploration.

In *Dhyana*, you become aware of your fullness, your connection between the individual consciousness and super-consciousness. When this connection is felt, there is no fear or frustration, because you realise that you are just an operator and an instrument of the Universe. Everything comes from the origin, from the mother-source.

So, in *Dhyana* you blend the three sheaths of time (past, present and future), into one single entity called presentness.

We started our journey from the heart, from the time we manifested ourselves in full physical form. Then, gradually, we moved up from the heart to the mind. After that, we became inattentive toward our heart, and became trapped in the web of the intellect. Here, in the mind, we are entertained, but not enlightened. In order to achieve enlightenment, we have to return to our hearts, or at least keep in touch with that original point from which we began our journey in this world. After this, we have to journey further into the innermost depth of our consciousness to experience the very essence of our being, the Self. Our evolution must parallel the evolution of the cosmos.

38
Life is Consciousness and Consciousness is Life

The outer universe is physical, whereas our individual inner universes are mystical. We all choose whether we progress in reaching the outer universe or in exploring the inner universe.

When you were first born, you were not fully aware of your existence. You expressed yourself instinctively. As a baby, you could only recognise your mother – and even that was not through the mind. That day became the first day of your conscious awareness on earth. As you grew, you gradually became aware of your existence, and you began to differentiate yourself from other beings. Then, you began to question your surroundings – everything that you saw, heard or read.

Later, because you wanted to make your life safe and secure, you cultivated your mind, and the mind sharpened into what we call intellect. Intellect allows us to arrange our lives on a material level. Science and technology, born out of our strong inquisitive minds, help us to live our lives in comfort. But putting such a strong emphasis on intellect, in the course of fulfilling our ever-increasing needs and necessities, leads us further from our hearts and our true nature. Without being aware of it, we become more and more materialistic over time.

After some time, you come to realise that acquiring material things is not the purpose of life. You cannot overcome your desires. You cannot even gain control of your own bodily functions or put reins on your mind. You are tossed here and there, a victim of circumstance and you begin to sense a void in your heart because precious moments of life are lost in only understanding and experiencing the superficial, external world. You become caught in the web and tentacles of society.

When you begin to cultivate your inner life, you realise that you are essentially greater than, and different from, outside objects upon which you have been spending time, energy and other resources. Ultimately, you look for permanent solutions and answers, which cannot be found in books because anything you read is someone else's experience, not your own personal experience. You may progress in the outside world by cultivating the power of the mind, or sharpening the intellect, but there is another surer and safer way forward.

We tend to believe that inner results are achieved primarily through physical action. We do not realise how silence can be even more powerful than action. In silence, you cease all voluntary physical activities. You become an observer on a journey to the centre of your existence. You strive to separate yourself from the mind, from the body and from the senses. They each have their own place, their own roles to play, but, as you keep observing, you have a powerful experience that you are different from your own mind, different from your own body, and that the senses are just tools. When you experience the difference, you are no longer affected by such illusions.

What is consciousness? Your whole being itself is consciousness. Intuition, intelligence, sensory abilities, reasoning and other faculties are all just extensions of consciousness. Life is consciousness. A lifeless body is only the debris of the departed conscious spirit.

You may call it *atma*. You may call it soul. But it is consciousness itself. You may add only one word: spirit – conscious spirit, or conscious Self. If you love someone, you do not just love his or her body. If you admire someone, it is not just his or her physical existence that you admire. The physical body alone cannot constitute a full living entity. The body cannot recognise itself. Only a living person can recognise himself or herself as a spirit. The body and the mind are the integration of many ingredients of consciousness itself. Life is consciousness and consciousness is life.

Though all people are conscious beings who have manifested themselves in physical form, they have no awareness that they are superior to their own body and mind. Why do some people not want to believe that they are different from what they have heard, seen and accepted? If one believes that one's existence is only physical, then one has to accept, believe and live with one's limitations, inabilities and incapacities. There is nothing higher to look for as a mere human without spiritual grace, without emotional experience and expression.

Perhaps you are wealthy, but still you may not be a materialist. If you allow materialism to overpower you, only then are you a materialist. If you can control materialism, you are a spiritual being. Human beings have made their lives artificial and mechanical, just keeping busy like ants and bees, with no time to spare, not even a few minutes, for their own inner progress.

From the poorest to the most affluent, we all want to find inner peace and know the truth of life. This tells us that achievement of worldly objectives is not the only purpose of life. Such achievements are only incidental.

Dhyana unfolds the mystical secrets and spiritual treasures of your consciousness. It unfolds gradually, layer by layer. There are many ways to expand one's consciousness.

Expansion of consciousness means expansion of your true inner nature. The more we expand our consciousness, the more we accommodate others. We invite them into our conscious periphery. We become oceanic because we see everyone in us. We discover and begin to experience the vastness of our own inner space.

Verbal explanation and silent experience are so far apart they are like the north and south poles. If you want explanation, you lose experience, and vice versa. Explanation must precede experience, because experience is the conclusion. Explanation cannot be the conclusion because explanation leaves you with doubt and negativity, whereas experience is settling.

Explanation and intellectual analysis should qualify us to gain spiritual experiences in the field of our inner consciousness. If we condition or limit our spiritual quest and search only for rational understanding, we feel a vacuum within us, whereby questions, doubt and anxiety may well linger in our minds. Hence spiritual inquiry must be two-fold. One aspect is the rational understanding of the inner Self, the higher Self, and their relation to the universe; and the other is silent spiritual experience. Only then will there be a fulfillment of our quest.

Glossary

Ananda: a high state of blissful experience between the conscious and unconscious mind.

Atma: spirit, consciousness or the Self.

Causal body: The body that has caused the human body; the first form of raw body, which has saturated itself in this gross body, but which will nevertheless maintain its individual identity.

Dhyana: deeply absorbed in nature; consciousness experienced through the heart; a state beyond what is normally deemed to be meditation.

Dhyani: truth-seeker, a practitioner of *Dhyana*.

Gross body: the whole living physical body.

Maya: the unreal, which competes with the real; the fence around truth; anything that is tempting and ephemeral but illusory, and yet creates an impression on the mind and senses.

Mysticism/Mystical: having to do with the mental level, halfway between the physical and spiritual, and often involving powers for the benefit of others. Mysticism is practical and direct spirituality, in which people attain indescribably beautiful and miraculous experiences. Here experience, rather than explanation, becomes the only reality. As an analogous example, a person who learns swimming and then becomes a master in swimming, could be considered the equivalent in that field to a spiritually enlightened person. If this swimmer can perform certain feats, save people from drowning, and inspire others to learn swimming, he would be a mystic. In the course of your journey to ultimate realisation, you achieve gifts of special faculties, allowing you to influence your own or someone else's destiny in a beneficial way. This is mysticism, but on this journey to the core of one's consciousness, *sadhakas* are often tempted and blocked by these gifts. Some become egoistic and a few others may misuse these gifts for power, position and wealth. Others are not side-tracked, and make further progress. Some are adventurous, take on their destiny and return to a normal level so that they may revive the potential of those mystical powers and live for others. They can also journey forward whenever they want to, to be one with super-consciousness. Mystics can be helpful to humanity, whereas those who are spiritually enlightened, without using mystical gifts, can only become a source of inspiration for others, rather than having the power to give it.

Physical: having to do with the world.

Pragnya: conscious awareness of oneself and of one's surroundings on a deeper level.

Prana/Pranic: life force, the pulse or vibration that is felt during the pause between inhalation and exhalation of breath.

Saaroogovum: is not a word from any language, but a sound and rhythm the author experienced while he was walking through woods in the morning just before sunrise. When he shared saaroogovum on the same day in the evening at the open audience, several members said their experiences were beautiful and elevating. Even today, on most occasions, Srinivas Arka begins and ends his open audiences with this mystic sound. In order to feel the benefits of its effects, one has to master the frequencies of its utterance and its right pronunciation in which one begins with a humming sound and concludes with the humming sound – a lingering nasal sound.

Sadhaka: a student/practitioner on the journey of personal evolution towards realisation.

Sadhana: a truth seeker's dedicated and consistent effort to realise the real by all possible spiritual means.

Subtle body: the body that dwells within the body on a micro-level, giving the momentum to the gross body to act and react.

Super-consciousness: higher consciousness, the origin of all conscious and unconscious manifestation.

Tapasya: Solitary spiritual discipline.

Srinivas Arka
Humble Books
P.O. Box 2217
London W1A 5GZ
United Kingdom

E-mail: HumbleBooks@aol.com

Toronto contact:
P.O. Box 92075
2900 Warden Avenue
Scarborough
Ontario
M1W 3Y8
Canada